PREMARITAL WORKBOOK FOR CHRISTIANS

PREMARITAL WORKBOOK *for* CHRISTIANS

EXERCISES AND REFLECTIONS TO PREPARE FOR A FAITH-BASED MARRIAGE

Dr. Chavonne Perotte

R

ROCKRIDGE PRESS

Scripture quotations are taken from the Holy Bible, New International Version®, NIV®. Copyright © 1973, 1978, 1984, 2011 by Biblica, Inc. Used by permission. All rights reserved worldwide.

Interior and Cover Designer: Scott Wooledge
Art Producer: Hannah Dickerson
Editor: Chloe Moffett
Production Editor: Jael Fogle
Production Manager: Martin Worthington

All illustrations used under license from The Noun Project and Shutterstock

Author photo courtesy of Jasmine Alston Photography

Paperback ISBN: 978-1-63807-931-6
eBook ISBN: 978-1-63807-625-4
R0

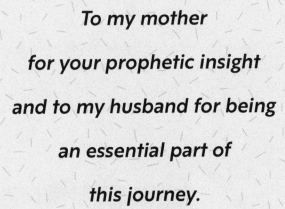

To my mother

for your prophetic insight

and to my husband for being

an essential part of

this journey.

CONTENTS

INTRODUCTION

Welcome! I am so excited for what's ahead for you in this workbook. Your investment of time, energy, and effort will pay off in the insights, wisdom, and understanding essential for creating a marriage that lasts. God is so pleased you are here doing this work. This workbook is for any couple preparing for marriage and can also be useful for couples who are already married and want to reestablish a strong foundation. This book is based in the Christian faith, as it references scripture and stories from the Bible, but its principles are applicable for couples of all faiths and religious beliefs. Marriage is a spiritual partnership, and that may look different from couple to couple.

There are endless advantages to having premarital guidance. Couples who go through this process enter marriage with fewer assumptions and have greater clarity on where each person stands on certain ideas related to their life together. They have a deeper understanding of each other and ready access to information that makes navigating the ups and downs of marriage much easier. The premarital counseling process helps you communicate more effectively, set realistic expectations, and make decisions together without unnecessary conflict. Seeking help at the start of your marriage can also normalize the idea of having an external support system to guide you as a couple, whether it be a marriage professional (coach, counselor, therapist) or a workbook like this.

The ideas and exercises in this workbook are informed by what I've seen work for my clients as a marriage coach and in my own ten-year marriage. From my training as a social science researcher and my experience developing relationship programs, I understand the dynamics of interpersonal communication and have created structures to help you be more self-aware and communicate openly and honestly with your partner.

In using this workbook, you will have conversations about your faith; the role of God in your marriage; your hopes, dreams, and goals as a couple; your roles in the marriage; expectations around money, work, children and parenting, communication, and conflict; establishing boundaries; family; friends; sex and intimacy; and spiritual growth. These are the most common topics that couples grapple with today, yet partners sometimes find themselves ill-equipped to effectively discuss these matters.

In each chapter, there is a guiding scripture and commentary along with exercises for you to complete. Consider this workbook a conversation tool to help you clarify your thoughts, document your ideas, and come to a mutual understanding of how you'd like your marriage to move forward. There is no right or wrong way to go through this workbook. You can jump around from topic to topic, or you can proceed chronologically.

I strongly encourage you to complete this workbook in its entirety and then flag any chapters you want to revisit regularly throughout your marriage. You will both grow and change over the years, and these discussion structures can be a wonderful guide in helping you grow and evolve your marriage just the same.

BEFORE YOU GET TO WORK

In order to get the most out of this book, there are some best practices to keep in mind, both in terms of logistics and in opening up the lines of communication and developing a deeper understanding of each other.

Logistically, it will be helpful to assign one of you as Partner A and the other as Partner B. This will help you always know which answers belong to whom for each question.

Establish a schedule for each of you. For example, you may choose to have one person complete their answers on Mondays, the other person complete their answers on Tuesdays, and both of you come together on Wednesdays to discuss. Or perhaps it works best for you to both respond and discuss in the same sitting. Decide now when and how you want to set aside time to work through this book. Choose a method that is convenient for both of you.

When coming up with your own personal responses, be honest. It will not be helpful to shape your answers based on what your partner says. Your experiences, thoughts, and ideas are equally valid, and transparency will help build a stronger foundation for your marriage.

When your partner is sharing their answers, set the intention to listen and understand. Do not interrupt to give your opinion or judge their answers. Approach each conversation with an open mind and heart. Your differences will ultimately help you both grow, and navigating those differences well makes your marriage stronger.

You might also consider using this book under the support and guidance of a marriage professional. If you are seeking formal premarital counseling/coaching or going through a premarital program at your church, feel free to share this resource and discuss the topics and your answers with that person.

CHAPTER 1

A God-Centered Marriage

> *And so we know and rely on the love God has for us.*
> *God is love. Whoever lives in love lives in God, and God in them.*
>
> **1 JOHN 4:16**

What brought you and your partner together? There are many ways to answer this question. For starters, you could focus on the circumstances that allowed you two to meet. Perhaps you were introduced by a friend, as was the case for my husband and me. Maybe you met online, at church, or at a social gathering. Perhaps you knew each other long ago and then reconnected via social media.

You might answer this question by describing the qualities and traits that attracted you to each other. Your similarities and shared values likely signaled to you that this was someone with whom you could successfully build a life. Perhaps you share a love of ministry and serving others. Maybe you are both ambitious individuals with big goals for your life. Or maybe you are both family-oriented and want to fill your home with loved ones.

You might also want to give the credit to God. Maybe your partner was the answer to a lot of prayer. You may say that God handpicked them for you and told you they were the one. It may be that, in obedience, you opened your heart to receive them, and you both felt led to one another by a power greater than the two of you. Perhaps, in your journey together, God has been speaking to you and revealing His plans for your union.

Whatever circumstances or factors brought you together initially, there is one thing that will *keep* you together through the different seasons of marriage. It is the center to which you must continually return and in which you must anchor yourself: love. I don't mean the conventional definition we often hear. This goes beyond the affection you may feel for one another. It's more than acting in ways that might be considered loving.

By "love," I mean *God's* love. God's love is more powerful than any love we as human beings could ever create on our own. It is a love that, in marriage, flows *through* us. We can love our partner unconditionally because *we* are loved unconditionally.

Creating a God-centered marriage means accessing God's love and relying on Him to be the source of the love you share with your partner. This is a love that never runs out. It's not something you must generate from your own willpower. It's something you only need to tap into because it's available all the time from the original source of love: God.

When you focus on God as the center of your marriage, you have His love and wisdom leading you through the ups and downs. His love is *in* you always. This scripture serves as a reminder of God's love. You can always operate out of love when you live in God and allow Him to live in you. Knowing and relying on God's love will create a marriage that lasts.

Elements of a God-Centered Marriage

Most Christians understand that God is the center of their lives. By extension, He is also the center of their marital relationship. God created marriage, and He has given us principles to live by so we can experience all that He intended through the marital covenant. Yet we don't always live this full-out every day. Simply *knowing* God is the center is not the same as God actively *being* the center. We, in our humanity, cannot consistently do the things our marriage requires (being patient, understanding, kind, forgiving). We need God to step in and give us His strength. We forget that God brought us together for His purposes and not just for our own desires.

Many couples enter marriage expecting their spouse to make their lives better and more fulfilling. They vaguely expect to have challenges, but when issues arise, they often blame each other rather than looking inside and changing themselves in order to better love each other. It's the latter approach that will make your marriage the way God designed it. Your marriage is a training ground for growing into who He created you to be.

Having a God-centered marriage means we seek His will and vision. We receive and agree with His desires for our hearts. We look for the ways He stretches us to grow. We adopt His model of unconditional love and acceptance by being committed to our partner even when they make mistakes or we disagree. We rely on His wisdom and insight to guide our interactions and decisions, even when our own emotions are not on board. We seek to glorify Him in how we live our lives together. In your marriage journey, imagine God being there to guide you in every moment. His Word has made you this promise: "Whether you turn to the right or to the left, your ears will hear a voice behind you, saying, 'This is the way; walk in it.'" (Isaiah 30:21)

 *Finding Your Center*

In the following exercise, you will discuss your own definitions of a God-centered marriage. You each may come to this conversation with different expectations and a different understanding of marriage. That is okay! The purpose of this exercise is to listen to each other and find ways to best support each other. Celebrate the places where you agree, and be open to understanding the places where you might disagree. Invite God in to help you find your unique way forward.

Complete each of the following statements with your honest thoughts and answers. Listen with an open mind as you both share your responses.

1. For me, a God-centered marriage looks like

Partner A: _____

Partner B: _____

2. I'll know I am achieving this when

Partner A: _____

Partner B: _____

3. I'll know I am *not* achieving this when

Partner A: _____

Partner B: _____

4. What will be easiest for me is

Partner A: _____

Partner B: _____

5. What will be hardest for me is

Partner A: _____

Partner B: _____

continued ➥

6. Ideally, I'd like for us both to work on this by

Partner A: _____

Partner B: _____

7. It's most important to me that we

Partner A: _____

Partner B: _____

8. To achieve that, I am willing to

Partner A: _____

Partner B: _____

9. The scripture or saying I will use as a guide in this area is

Partner A: _____

Partner B: _____

10. I want to have a God-centered marriage because

Partner A: _____

Partner B: _____

God's Love and Yours

I don't think our human minds can truly comprehend how much God loves us. The more you understand and receive God's love for you, the greater capacity you'll have to express that love to your spouse. The more you have experienced love, the more you can give and receive love. As God's child, this is not contingent on how much love you have received from others in your life. Instead, it's proportional to how much you understand and receive God's love.

When was the last time you paused and allowed yourself to just soak up God's love for you? Do it now. Feel the abundance and limitlessness of it. Allow its warmth to flood your heart. Bring to your awareness how nothing you do or say could ever diminish the love God has for you. Feel His love abiding in you. Every mistake, every time you fall short, every moment you ignore Him, He is there, loving you unconditionally.

This context is important when it comes to grasping the magnitude of what it means to love your partner. God's love is a selfless, sacrificial love rooted in service. Jesus models this for us and explicitly tells us what to do: "A new command I give you: Love one another. As I have loved you, so you must love one another." (John 13:34) Your marriage is the most obvious place for you to live out this commandment. You can only operate fully in obedience to God when you truly understand His love for you.

Love as God Loves

Each of you will come to this marriage with a different understanding and experience of love. The following exercise offers a wonderful opportunity to talk about that. Use the following prompts to rate your level of agreement with each statement. Partner A should indicate their response by circling the appropriate number. Partner B should indicate their response by placing an asterisk by the appropriate number. As you rate your answers for each of the following questions, discuss why you gave the answer you did.

1. On a scale of 1 to 10, I am able to experience God's love:

    NOT MUCH AT ALL   A GREAT DEAL

    1   2   3   4   5   6   7   8   9   10

2. My ability to express love is:

    NOT MUCH AT ALL   A GREAT DEAL

    1   2   3   4   5   6   7   8   9   10

3. My ability to receive love is:

    NOT MUCH AT ALL   A GREAT DEAL

    1   2   3   4   5   6   7   8   9   10

4. Our relationship is currently centered on God's love:

    NOT MUCH AT ALL   A GREAT DEAL

    1   2   3   4   5   6   7   8   9   10

5. I am able to understand what it means to love like God:

    NOT MUCH AT AL   A GREAT DEAL

    1   2   3   4   5   6   7   8   9   10

TAKEAWAYS

God is the source of the love in your marriage. Understanding God's love for you helps you love your partner more fully. When you run into challenges and issues, turn to God for insight and wisdom.

Talk It Over

- What's the biggest benefit of having a God-centered marriage?

- What is your understanding of God's love for you?

- When are the times you question God's love? How does that impact your relationship with Him?

- When are the times you question your partner's love? How does that affect the way you love them in return?

- What would it look like to truly love each other the way God loves you? What are the things you would start doing more? What are the things you would do less?

- What are the things that could potentially take you off track?

- How can you best handle those off-track moments?

- What can you do to regularly understand and be filled with God's love? How can you support each other in that?

Keep in Mind

- God is a perfect example of unconditional love.

- The goal in marriage is to love the way God loves.

- The more you receive and understand God's love, the more you'll be able to love each other well.

Next Steps

- Spend five to ten minutes each week coming up with evidence of God's love for you.

- Identify two new ways to love your partner the way God loves you.

- List one way God can help you love when your human emotions, like anger and frustration, get in the way.

CHAPTER 2

Making the Commitment

> *"Write down the revelation and make it plain on tablets."*
>
> HABAKKUK 2:2

> *"Therefore, what God has joined together, let no one separate."*
>
> MATTHEW 19:6

> *The one who doubts is like a wave of the sea, blown and tossed by the wind . . .*
> *Such a person is double-minded and unstable in all they do.*
>
> JAMES 1:6, 8

Be clear. Be decided. Be steady. These three verses show us how to create commitment in marriage.

You must first be clear. Having clarity means you understand that in marriage, you are committing yourself to choosing your partner in good times and bad, and to consistently look for ways to solve issues rather than allowing them to be excuses to leave. While no one can predict all that life may bring, you want to be clear about the things you do know now, such as any differences in values, priorities, or goals for your life together. You want to enter this sacred union having done the work of being honest, transparent, and authentic. You must know yourself and be able to show yourself to your partner fully.

The two of you are creating a vision for your life with one another, which means you're working toward certain goals, experiences, and purposes together. Assumptions and unspoken expectations, like assuming your spouse views work/life balance the way you do or expecting to contribute equally to household responsibilities, cover up the clarity you need to sustain that vision. You can't honestly commit to what you don't understand. Knowing what God wants for you and the reason He brought you together creates the perfect foundation to keep pushing through, even when times get hard.

Once you are clear, you must be decided. Nothing can tear apart a marriage that God has ordained and put together. When you are decided, you can take what you've learned from gaining clarity and apply it in moments that lack clarity, sustaining your marriage over the long haul. I often look at the wedding photo of my husband and myself walking back down the aisle after our vows. That couple had no idea what challenges and issues they would face. Yet they decided to stay the course and become the couple we are ten years later, with a lot of unknowns along the way.

God is certain, but He is giving you the decision. When you operate with that level of decisiveness, nothing will lead you to seriously question your marriage or abandon it. Not even you can separate it, even if your thoughts and feelings lead you to believe it's not working. Entering this covenant means that God is the leader, always providing the way for you to work things out.

Lastly, making the commitment to get married requires a one-track mind. You cannot vacillate on whether this is the right thing or the wrong thing. When you are double-minded you will always sway with the wind, moving toward or away from your partner depending on the circumstances. In your marriage, there will be hard moments where you will need the Lord to guide you. You must believe that He is giving you the answer and not doubt. If your marriage is God's design, you can rest knowing the answer to remaining committed is always yes. You can be steady in that.

What Commitment Means to You

I often witness couples who have different ideas about commitment. Typically, when couples marry, they have a simple and surface-level understanding of commitment, so it's easy to say they commit to being together forever. They don't know what challenges they will face, and they commit to each other when the relationship is going very well.

Over time, however, this commitment may be called into question when their differences are hard to navigate, when someone violates an important expectation, or if they just drift apart and no longer enjoy each other. They haven't fully considered that one person might be ready to un-commit before the other. This is devastating for the partner who's still willing to do the work. They take their partner's lack of commitment personally. But here's what I want you to know: Someone else's level of commitment has nothing to do with you. It has everything to do with their own beliefs and experiences.

Commitment is a subjective concept. One person may think commitment to marriage means being home every day by a certain time and scheduling regular date nights. Another person may think commitment means just deciding you won't ever leave. Neither is right or wrong. They are just different. Take stock of your overall relationship with commitment. What has commitment looked like for you professionally? Do you change jobs frequently? What does commitment look like for you in friendships? Do you have longtime friends? What are the factors that led you to be uncommitted to something you once agreed to?

 ## Why Commit?

There are many different reasons to be committed in a marriage; over time, you may need them all. In the following exercise, you will create your own definitions of what commitment looks like to you and explore the various forms of commitment you may adopt throughout your relationship. Complete the following statements and then share with your partner.

1. Being committed because **I want** to be in this marriage looks like
Example: Making an effort to spend time together and engage my partner in doing things we can both enjoy.

Partner A: _____

_____

Partner B: _____

_____

2. Being committed because **I honor my vows** to this marriage looks like

Partner A: _____

_____

Partner B: _____

_____

continued ➡

3. Being committed because **I love and care for my partner** in this marriage looks like

Partner A: _____

_____

Partner B: _____

_____

4. Being committed because **I believe in the future** of this marriage looks like

Partner A: _____

_____

Partner B: _____

_____

5. Being committed because **I choose to obey God** in this marriage looks like

Partner A: _____

_____

Partner B: _____

_____

The Promises You'll Keep

What are you really promising to do as you embark on your marriage? Regardless of what you say in your wedding vows, it's important to understand what you're agreeing to give your relationship for a *lifetime*.

Right now, you seem like a great match. You have likely already made it through some conflicts or obstacles. As discussed earlier (page 10), it's easy to promise to commit when things are going well. But I want to help you be committed now for the promises you haven't yet needed to make. To do that, you will need to understand the areas you believe might strain or break your marriage. Every marriage goes through growing and stretching seasons. But when you understand your own personal commitments and decide now that you'll remain committed, your marriage has a much greater chance of rebounding from these setbacks.

Each of us has our boundaries and things we cannot accept in a marriage. I encourage you to discuss your own deal-breakers and why they are important standards for you. Abuse and infidelity are two common examples of boundaries that should not get crossed in a healthy marriage.

 ## Avoiding Deal-Breakers

Following are a series of challenging circumstances that might test one's commitment to marriage. Using the range of 1–10 (where 1 is most problematic and 10 is least problematic), rank in order the degree to which the statement represents a deal-breaker for you. As you share your answers, discuss in detail why you responded the way you did. Where are your responses similar? Where do your thoughts differ?

I will be committed to you and this marriage, even when:

Partner A   Partner B

Partner A	Partner B	
		We argue and can't get along.
		You make decisions without involving me.
		We don't agree on important decisions (money, parenting, extended family, home, where to live, etc.).
		We don't agree on how we practice our faith.
		You do or say things that hurt my feelings.
		You are not putting forth as much effort as I think you should.
		I feel lonely or neglected.
		You act in ways I don't agree with.
		You blame me for things that are not my fault.
		I don't feel your love in the way I want it most.

TAKEAWAYS

Committing to a shared vision of marriage with God at the center will keep your relationship intact even when it is shaken. There will always be challenging circumstances, but deciding ahead of time what you will give to keep your commitment strong is very helpful in weathering those storms.

Talk It Over

· What things are you already doing that support your commitment to each other?

· Why is it helpful for you to look at commitment from several different angles?

· What resources or supports can you turn to when commitment wanes?

· In what ways is God a great example of what committed love looks like?

· What's something you personally need to do to keep your commitment strong?

Keep in Mind

· Commitment looks different for everyone and there are many different reasons to remain committed.

· It's important to understand what you are committing to and your reasons for wanting to be committed.

· Commitment is a decision that can be maintained even when times are hard and your marriage feels difficult.

Next Steps

· Write out a vision for your marriage, then submit it to God in prayer. Revisit this vision every six months and adjust it as God gives you insight and wisdom.

· Identify three qualities of your personality that will help you remain committed to your marriage.

· Think about your biggest deal-breaker and share it with your partner. Discuss why this is so important to you.

CHAPTER 3

Your Marriage Goals

May he give you the desire of your heart and make all your plans succeed.

PSALM 20:4

Everyone enters marriage with expectations and dreams of what their life will be like. This is often shaped, for good or bad, by what we experienced growing up, what we saw on TV, or our interpretations of things people have told us. You may have your own ideas about the ideal amount of time spent together, childcare, how to make financial decisions, or celebrating holidays. There is nothing inherently wrong with that. However, when we have certain images in our mind that we've never questioned, we can idealize marriage in ways that are not helpful.

God is the first stop when creating marriage goals. What does He want for you individually and as a couple? We all come to relationships with a preference for certain experiences. Some people want a lot of closeness and connection; others prefer to live more independently. Some people like to plan for the future; others enjoy a more spontaneous existence. You want a partnership that honors who you are and helps you both grow and experience all that God has for you together.

What might God be placing in your heart for your marriage? What do you want to feel, do, and have together as a couple? It's important to discern whether these things are aligned with God's purpose and plans for you. God is always interested in the highest good for everyone. He will place His desires in your heart, and, as a result, you will want them, too. That's alignment. God is not a genie in a bottle here to fulfill our wants. His ways are not our ways, and He has foresight that we could never have. Our lives work best when we seek what He has planned for us and want His will more than our own.

I have often prayed and asked God to remove any desires I had that didn't align with His will for my life. For example, I started my coaching practice while on maternity leave with my first child. I struggled to find the right balance between my own ambition and my desire to be a present mother. I knew enough to trust God and seek His insight and wisdom, guiding me and showing me when my focus needed to be at home. It is not always easy to trade your desires for God's, but I encourage you to make it a practice. There is nothing better than wanting the same thing for your life and marriage that God wants. When God is behind your goals, you can never, ever fail.

There will be situations where you won't clearly know what God wants for you as a couple. Don't worry! He is always looking at your heart. When you seek to please Him first, He will come in and "establish your plans" (Proverbs 16:3), meaning that He will put them in a favorable position. Even if you are not taking the absolute right next step, God will position it according to His will. He will work all things for your good (Romans 8:28).

Debunking Marriage Myths

There are infinite ideas, advice, and myths out there for what makes a happy marriage. When couples are ill-informed about the realities of building a life together, it gives birth to unrealistic expectations and opens the door to disappointment. In the early, romantic stages, it's easy to believe it should be that way all the time, and then just as quickly decide a marriage is doomed when the romance fades.

It's important to separate what's true and acceptable for you from myths perpetuated by society and others. There is no one, right way to have a marriage. There is only the marriage that you make right for you. There is no one way a spouse should think, feel, and act. There is only the spouse you are committed to loving and accepting, even when they are imperfect. Here are some common myths I often see operating under the surface of marriages that create unnecessary hardship.

- You have to be on the same page all the time.
- It's your spouse's responsibility to make you happy and meet all your needs.
- Marriage should always feel fun, passionate, and exciting.
- Being married will automatically make your life better.
- Good marriages only happen when two people are compatible and get along easily.
- You should never go to bed feeling angry at each other.
- You have to talk about all your issues until you solve them.

These marriage myths can shape your expectations in ways that make getting along and enjoying the marriage you have almost impossible. I encourage you to challenge some of the things you hear about marriage, and enter your union with an open mind.

Myth vs. Reality

Not all marriage myths are black and white. Often, the intention behind a marriage myth is positive. As a couple, you want to determine which ideas will help your marriage and which will potentially hurt it. The following exercise will help you discuss some common marriage myths and come to a greater understanding of how you would like to operate together. For each of the following myths, discuss why it is a myth and what you'd like for your marriage instead.

MYTH	WHY THIS IS A MYTH	WHAT WE'D LIKE FOR OUR MARRIAGE
You have to be on the same page all the time.		
It's your spouse's responsibility to make you happy and meet all your needs.		
Marriage should always feel fun, passionate, and exciting.		
Being married will automatically make your life better.		
Good marriages only happen when two people are compatible and get along easily.		
You can never go to bed feeling angry at each other.		
You have to talk about all your issues until you solve them.		

Sharing Your Hopes and Dreams

The unique hopes and dreams you bring to your marriage are beautiful things, especially when they align with God's design. Your marriage can be a safe place for you to explore your purpose and fulfill your potential here on Earth. Having support, encouragement, and insight from your partner is an amazing experience and can help you become who you were created to be. Advancing your hopes and dreams as a couple is another gift marriage offers. When you build dreams together, you create more moments of meaningful connection and relational intimacy. As you form your own family unit, you create a new vision for your future.

That said, I want to normalize the possibility that there will be seasons in your marriage where you don't see things the same way or have the same dreams. That's okay. It does not mean your spouse is against you, or that you are somehow not meant to be together. You can always find a way to move forward and create room for those differences to coexist. There will be times when God may give a dream to one of you that the other doesn't understand. The key is to continue to honor each other, and not convince or force the other person to get on board. If God intends something for your life, it will happen. He will bring your partner along at the right time. In the meantime, be sure you are operating out of God's will. You can still love and be committed to each other, even in the moments when it looks like you might be on different paths.

The key in sharing your hopes and dreams is being open, understanding each other, encouraging each other, and building each other up (1 Thessalonians 5:11). When you can both do this, your marriage will thrive and the right hopes and dreams will become reality.

 A Dream to Build a Marriage On

The following exercise will help you share some of your hopes and dreams. For each of the following prompts, write your honest answers. Review your responses together once you're finished. While listening to your partner, be open, encouraging, and accepting.

1. What is a dream you had as a child?

Partner A: _____

_____

Partner B: _____

_____

2. What is a dream you don't often talk about?

Partner A: _____

_____

Partner B: _____

_____

3. What is a dream you are actively working toward right now?

Partner A: _____

_____

Partner B: _____

_____

4. What is a dream you have for your life as a couple/family?

Partner A: _____

_____

Partner B: _____

_____

5. What is a dream you believe God has placed in your heart?

Partner A: _____

_____

Partner B: _____

_____

continued ➡

6. What is a dream you want to help your partner pursue?

Partner A: _____

_____

Partner B: _____

_____

Setting Meaningful Goals

Setting goals together is a necessary step for achieving any dream you want to accomplish. Goals are specific, measurable ideas on which you can take action. For example, your dream may be to own a home together. A goal might be to save $15,000 within twelve months. Your marriage goals are the stepping stones to making your dreams a reality.

Few couples actually spend time thinking about goals for their marriage. People often come to marriage assuming they think the same way and are working toward the same things, or they wind up pursuing separate goals and ultimately separate lives. Being proactive with your goals will help you stay on track together.

There are no right or wrong goals for your marriage. Each of you may approach marriage goals from a different perspective. You may have individual goals that impact your marriage and goals as a couple. Goals may fall into a number of categories, including:

- Financial
- Social (friends and family)
- Physical health
- Professional
- Educational
- Family/parenting

- Emotional
- Personal growth
- Spiritual
- Intimacy
- Vacation/leisure
- Home ownership/location

It's okay for each of you to have different priorities. The greatest gift you can give to your partner is to take responsibility for the goals you care about most. If it's important to you that your savings account always be at a certain number, *you* own that task. If your partner prioritizes socializing with family and friends, they can own that part of your relationship. Goals and priorities are an opportunity to tap into the best parts of each of you, rather than creating conflict and division.

Separate Goals, Together

The following exercise will help you to set and share goals together. Having a combination of short- and long-term goals will help you stay focused on the present, while building a foundation for lifelong dreams.

Complete each of the following statements and share your responses with your partner. Notice where your priorities are similar and where they differ.

1. One of the most important personal goals you're working on right now is

Partner A: _____

Partner B: _____

This is very important to you because

Partner A: _____

Partner B: _____

Accomplishing this goal will benefit your marriage by

Partner A: _____

Partner B: _____

One of your most important personal goals for the future is

Partner A: _____

Partner B: _____

This is very important to you because

Partner A: _____

Partner B: _____

continued ➡

Accomplishing this goal will benefit your marriage by

Partner A: _____

Partner B: _____

One of the most important goals for you as a couple right now is

Partner A: _____

Partner B: _____

This is very important to you because

Partner A: _____

Partner B: _____

Accomplishing this goal will benefit your marriage by

Partner A: _____

Partner B: _____

One of the most important goals for you as a couple in the future is

Partner A: _____

Partner B: _____

This is very important to you because

Partner A: _____

Partner B: _____

Accomplishing this goal will benefit your marriage by

Partner A: _____

Partner B: _____

TAKEAWAYS

The hopes and dreams in your heart are wonderful opportunities for you to support each other as a couple. It's important to distinguish between the desires and goals that come from God and any ideas and myths inherited from others or society. Remember that when you are focusing on God's will for your life and committed to keeping Him front and center, it will be easier to resolve your conflicts and accomplish your dreams for your marriage.

Talk It Over

- What's a mistake you might have made if you hadn't discussed the questions in this chapter?

- How are you on the same page about goals and dreams?

- How can you support each other when you want different things?

- How will you involve God as you make plans and take action toward your goals?

- What concerns do you have about the best way to balance your individual goals and your priorities as a couple?

Keep in Mind

- Marriage myths can create unrealistic expectations that prevent you from enjoying the marriage you have.

- Your marriage can be a great environment for fulfilling your personal goals and dreams while also creating a dream life together.

- Goals are the specific milestones you will hit to achieve your dreams, and they fall into a broad range of categories.

Next Steps

- Define three specific elements of what a happy marriage looks like to you without adopting marriage myths that are unrealistic.

- Schedule a regular date (e.g., January 1) to review your hopes and dreams each year and adjust them as needed.

- Identify one specific way you will encourage and hold each other accountable as you work to achieve your personal and marriage goals.

CHAPTER 4

Who Does What?

> *Just as a body, though one, has many parts, but all its many parts form one body,*
> *so it is with Christ ... But in fact God has placed the parts in the body, every one of*
> *them, just as he wanted them to be. If they were all one part, where would the*
> *body be?*
>
> 1 CORINTHIANS 12:12, 18–19

God is so wise. He creates everything in perfect order. From how He created the world to how He designed our bodies, the interdependence of all things is intentional.

Many times couples come together because of their perceived similarities only to later be frustrated by their differences. They spend a lot of time wishing their partners thought or acted more like them. But just as our bodies are made up of different parts that serve different functions, your differences can work together to strengthen you as a unit. Maybe one person is inclined to keep things very tidy and plan ahead, while the other is able to bring levity to conversations and diffuse tension. Perhaps one of you is good at tracking spending, while the other plans family outings and keeps relationships intact. Recognizing these tendencies as assets to your marriage rather than qualities you'd like to change will make all the difference in how you work together.

Honoring your different priorities will also help you define your roles more easily. As discussed in chapter 3 (page 17), you should try to take the lead on things you like to take care of. These roles can then be ones you wholeheartedly embrace rather than causing resentment because your spouse does not prioritize them to the degree that you do. For example, if you like your home very neat and tidy, you can be the one to organize the cleaning or create a family chore chart. Create a system that works for you and take responsibility for making sure it happens. Remember, there is no right way to have a marriage. You just have to make it right for you.

Who does what in a marriage represents an important set of decisions that creates the foundation for realistic expectations. If you agree to perform some specific duty, it's as if you are saying to your partner, "You can count on me to do this." It is important to be honest and clear about the things you will be happy to do or committed to do. If circumstances change, be quick to communicate that those specific roles no longer work or make sense.

If your spouse is no longer fulfilling a role they once agreed to, instead of being upset and frustrated with them, be caring. Ask if expecting them to do it is still realistic. Be willing to find new ways of getting things done that really work and don't just leave you with more to do. There are creative ways to handle the responsibilities of your life that still enlist the help of others.

Your relationship roles will be an evolving conversation. Experiment. Try it one way, evaluate, and then make adjustments. This will help you avoid unnecessary arguments and hurt feelings. Keep in mind that the two of you are coming together for the first time to develop and carry out an intricate long-term project together—your life.

The Unique Qualities You Bring to the Relationship

Your unique, individual qualities can support the success of your marriage. How wonderful it is that God knit your inmost being and designed you to be one of a kind (Psalm 139:13–14). The same holds true for your partner. What's important is that you honor what makes you unique and that you are both committed to bringing your qualities together for the good of the marriage. For example, if you tend to be more sensitive to others' feelings, use that to help your marriage instead of shaming yourself for your emotions. If you value structure and discipline but your partner is more spontaneous, you don't need to reshape yourself to be just like them. Instead, find a balance that honors who you are and moves the marriage forward.

You may also have some unique qualities that could potentially strain your marriage. It's important to be aware of these, too. I like to offer these three perspectives: what's good for you, what's good for your partner, and what's best for the marriage. This will help you assess if your behavior is helping or hurting your marriage. When one person is set in their ways and unwilling to compromise, it's harder for their partner to connect and communicate with them.

Because you are human, your marriage will bring out the best and the worst in you. But keep in mind that God's spirit dwells within you, and you can embody His goodness and love when you are willing to view yourself in the best possible light. I've heard many people say, "I'm not the kind of person to . . ." and then list all the limiting beliefs they have about themselves. In marriage, expand the box you use to define yourself so you can show up as your best. Let your uniqueness shine, and make sure it supports the kind of marriage you want to have.

 ## *Appreciate Your Differences*

The following exercise will help you determine how your unique qualities impact your relationship. In part one, you will take stock of how your qualities can strengthen your marriage. In part two, you'll share some of the ways they may challenge it.

PART ONE

Partner A

I'm really good at _____

I really enjoy _____

It's very important to me that _____

I am the kind of person to _____

I always want to _____

This can really help our relationship because _____

_____

Partner B

I'm really good at _____

I really enjoy _____

It's very important to me that _____

continued ▶

I am the kind of person to _____

I always want to _____

This can really help our relationship because _____

_____

PART TWO

Partner A

I'm not very good at _____

I don't enjoy _____

I have a hard time _____

I can sometimes _____

I never want to _____

This could potentially make our relationship harder because _____

_____

Partner B

I'm not very good at _____

I don't enjoy _____

I have a hard time _____

I can sometimes _____

I never want to _____

This could potentially make our relationship harder because _____

_____

Discuss your answers. In what ways are you a great match for each other? What differences will you need to be intentional about appreciating?

Relationship Roles

It's important that you understand the roles you will take on in your marriage and develop a common definition of that term. A role can be a responsibility, expectation, or task. It's deciding someone's part in something or the position or purpose they have. God has designed you to naturally be attracted to certain roles in your marriage. Notice what they might be, and seek His help in carrying out whatever roles you ultimately agree to hold.

However you choose to define roles in your relationship, be clear about the specific things you will or will not be doing. For example, in my own marriage, I have the role of meal provider. This does not mean I always have to cook. It means I am responsible for making sure we all have something to eat. This might mean that one day I cook, one day I pick up something, and another day I ask my husband to cook or pick up something. Because this is my role, my husband expects me to be the leader here. As a result, he dedicates his time and attention to other aspects of our life that I pay less attention to. It doesn't matter which roles you take on, as long as they work for you and the relationship is fair and balanced.

Roles are not rules. They exist to help you work together. In a marriage there will be times where roles get blurred and it's not clear who is supposed to do what. In these instances, take a learning approach. Look for what's creating the breakdown and focus on solutions rather than placing blame. You don't want to get into the habit of policing each other. You are a team working toward the same goal. Be careful not to assume ill intent and be gracious to each other as you continue to clarify and solidify your roles.

 *Role with It*

Following is a list of common roles within marriage. For each, have a conversation about who will assume leadership and who will take the supporting role, and identify what some specific responsibilities might be for each.

continued ➡

Write the leader's and supporter's names in their respective columns and list the things each one will do in that role. Feel free to discuss other roles not covered. Revisit this list and modify it as your circumstances change over time.

ROLE	AS THE LEADER, I WILL	AS THE SUPPORTER, I WILL
Example: Paying bills	*Alex: check the mail for bills, set up online payment profiles, schedule payments*	*Sam: make sure a percentage of my paycheck goes into our joint account to cover my contribution*
Paying bills		
Spiritual/faith		
Budgeting/saving		
Cleaning the home		
Food/meals		
Relationship nurturing/growth		
Children		
Cars		
Home decorating		
Home maintenance/upkeep		
Fun/leisure		
Extended family/friends		

Making Team Decisions

As we've discussed in this chapter, each of you has a role to play, even if you are not the official "leader" in a particular aspect of your life. God values teamwork: "Two are better than one, because they have a good return for their labor: If either of them falls down, one can help the other up" (Ecclesiastes 4:9–10).

As you approach decisions, be clear about your position and what kinds of decisions you want to be involved in. Don't leave your partner to assume where you stand. As you bring ideas to each other, spend time thinking about how you will handle things when you don't agree. Praying about how to handle disagreements is very helpful. Sometimes there is no clear middle ground, but God has the answer and is always there to provide clarity.

For some couples, having to make decisions together feels hard. One person may make quick decisions, while another takes more time to think things through. Neither is right or wrong. Knowing each other's preferences can help make the process more effective. For example, if you like to make fast decisions, you might give your partner a time frame and the reasons behind it. If you like to think things over, be clear about when you will get back to your partner.

Self-awareness is also important when it comes to making decisions as a couple. What might keep you from talking with your partner about a decision? Are you afraid they won't agree? That they might try to take over? That they may not get a say? If you find yourself not wanting to communicate about decisions openly, get curious as to why. Then evaluate whether making the decision on your own or together is best for your marriage.

Getting Involved

How strongly do you want to be involved in each type of decision? Use the following prompts to rate your level of agreement with the importance of discussing the item together *before* a decision is made. Partner A should indicate their response by circling the appropriate number. Partner B should indicate their response by placing an asterisk by the appropriate number. As you review your answers, discuss why you gave the answers you did. The point is to get a clear perspective on what you both want to talk about.

1. Investments or purchases over $500

STRONGLY DISAGREE							STRONGLY AGREE		
1	2	3	4	5	6	7	8	9	10

continued ➡

2. Ongoing subscriptions for services

STRONGLY DISAGREE · · · · · · · · STRONGLY AGREE

1   2   3   4   5   6   7   8   9   10

3. Changes to our schedule or normal routine

STRONGLY DISAGREE · · · · · · · · STRONGLY AGREE

1   2   3   4   5   6   7   8   9   10

4. What we eat for meals

STRONGLY DISAGREE · · · · · · · · STRONGLY AGREE

1   2   3   4   5   6   7   8   9   10

5. When to have children

STRONGLY DISAGREE · · · · · · · · STRONGLY AGREE

1   2   3   4   5   6   7   8   9   10

6. Job transitions (quitting or changing positions)

STRONGLY DISAGREE · · · · · · · · STRONGLY AGREE

1   2   3   4   5   6   7   8   9   10

7. New activities that require additional time (clubs, ministries, hobbies)

STRONGLY DISAGREE · · · · · · · · STRONGLY AGREE

1   2   3   4   5   6   7   8   9   10

8. Home improvement projects

STRONGLY DISAGREE · · · · · · · · STRONGLY AGREE

1   2   3   4   5   6   7   8   9   10

9. Activities or events for the children

STRONGLY DISAGREE · · · · · · · · STRONGLY AGREE

1   2   3   4   5   6   7   8   9   10

10. People hired for services (babysitters, contractors, etc.)

STRONGLY DISAGREE · · · · · · · · STRONGLY AGREE

1   2   3   4   5   6   7   8   9   10

11. Activities with friends/family

STRONGLY DISAGREE · · · · · · · · STRONGLY AGREE

1   2   3   4   5   6   7   8   9   10

TAKEAWAYS

Your marriage can be a wonderful combination of your best qualities as unique individuals. The life you build together will require your different approaches and ways of thinking. The more you are able to appreciate the gifts and perspectives you each bring, the better you'll be able to make decisions and operate as leaders in your respective roles. With each of you playing to your strengths and respecting each other's, you'll be more successful in achieving your God-ordained goals for your lives and your marriage.

Talk It Over

- What are you walking away with after having gone through this chapter?

- What roles are you most clear about and committed to?

- About what decisions do you feel most comfortable talking to your partner? About what do you feel least comfortable?

- Do you feel your responsibilities in the marriage truly represent your best?

- Which of your roles makes you feel most valued?

Keep in Mind

- You and your partner are unique, and you will play different roles in your marriage.

- Your differences will help you make your partnership stronger when you see them as assets.

- Being a leader in a particular area involves taking responsibility and engaging your partner to be a valuable supporter.

Next Steps

- Identify two great qualities you and your partner have been gifted with and how they can help your marriage thrive.

- Set a monthly check-in and evaluate if your current roles and responsibilities are working and realistic for the two of you.

- Come up with one specific way you will create a team spirit in your marriage.

CHAPTER 5

Money

Command those who are rich in this present world not to be arrogant nor to put their hope in wealth, which is so uncertain, but to put their hope in God, who richly provides us with everything for our enjoyment. Command them to do good, to be rich in good deeds, and to be generous and willing to share. In this way they will lay up treasure for themselves as a firm foundation for the coming age, so that they may take hold of the life that is truly life.

1 TIMOTHY 6:17–19

There are so many strong opinions when it comes to money. As believers, we are taught that money is the root of all evil and to not make money our god. Many of these scriptures are preached without the proper context, leaving people with the idea that wanting or having a lot of money is ungodly. Here, I want to offer the idea that money is a tool, a resource we have access to here on earth to take care of ourselves, our lives, and our aspirations. We need it to survive. Money itself is neutral and can be used for good or harm.

The scripture from 1 Timothy offers a view into how people who have money can use that money for good and be generous. As we are God's children, He is the source of all the money we will ever need. He provides us with the skills, abilities, and opportunities to create wealth (Deuteronomy 8:18). Therefore, when it comes to the money we may want or desire, our focus must first be on the God who helps us obtain money. God is glorified when we use our money in honorable ways.

I've seen so many couples struggle when it comes to money. Whether it's not having enough, not agreeing on how to use it, or how long and hard one has to work to earn it, beliefs about money and its influence in a marriage are palpable. If, as tradition has dictated in the past, one spouse is expected to be the primary provider, it can sometimes send that person into a frenzy of overworking to provide at the level they would like. In other instances, one partner might make much more money than the other, which could lead to resentment.

Consider the possibility that you and your partner do not have to struggle in this area. This chapter will help clear a path forward. As we discuss money in the following pages, I want to invite you to see money in a new way, to understand your own money story, and to recognize that you can have conversations and make decisions about money together from a grounded place.

The goal is to find what will be true for you as a couple, untangled from the opinions of others. Your views about money will change over time as you enter seasons of having more or less. No matter the circumstances, it's important that you both remain anchored in God as the source and ultimate provider.

Your Relationship to Money

Money is one of those hot topics in life—and in marriage—where strong opinions, emotional reactions, and traumatic experiences all come together. Why is that? What comes up for you when you think about how you like to use your money? There is no right or wrong, just what's true for you.

You can have a relationship with money just as you have relationships with people. This perspective was incredibly helpful for me as I uncovered my own relationship with money and its impact on my marriage. My husband is more of a saver and prefers to use money to establish financial opportunities for the future. He is more disciplined in day-to-day spending. I am much more of an in-the-moment spender, and I used money based on what brought me fun and joy. I didn't plan much and didn't want to think about saving for the future.

After coming to a greater understanding of how I related to money, I could see why I felt tense and inadequate whenever we'd have money conversations. It wasn't about him at all; it was about me and how I saw money in my life. Using the concept discussed in chapter 4, I began to ask, "What would be best for our marriage?" I subsequently adjusted my relationship with money to support the kind of marriage I wanted to have.

Your differences in how you view money can actually serve your relationship as you balance each other out. But first, you must assess your relationship with money as an individual and determine if it is healthy. Any extreme relationship with money can be harmful. Savers can operate from total scarcity, and spenders can operate from complete carelessness. Here we will do the work to find a great middle ground for you both.

Is Your Spending Healthy?

The following exercise will help you uncover more about your relationship with money. For each of the following statements, consider how much time you spend thinking or acting in that way. Then rate the degree to which you believe your current thinking or behaviors are healthy. Use the following 1–10 scale, where Partner A indicates their response with a circle, and Partner B indicates their response by placing an asterisk next to the selected number.

1. "I think about making money so I can spend it and enjoy myself in the moment."

NOT HEALTHY AT ALL   EXTREMELY HEALTHY

1   2   3   4   5   6   7   8   9   10

2. "I worry about having more money."

NOT HEALTHY AT ALL   EXTREMELY HEALTHY

1   2   3   4   5   6   7   8   9   10

3. "I feel grateful for the money I do have."

NOT HEALTHY AT ALL   EXTREMELY HEALTHY

1   2   3   4   5   6   7   8   9   10

4. "I find myself talking positively about money."

NOT HEALTHY AT ALL   EXTREMELY HEALTHY

1   2   3   4   5   6   7   8   9   10

5. "I feel afraid to use the money I have."

NOT HEALTHY AT ALL   EXTREMELY HEALTHY

1   2   3   4   5   6   7   8   9   10

6. "I work so that I can have more money."

NOT HEALTHY AT ALL   EXTREMELY HEALTHY

1   2   3   4   5   6   7   8   9   10

7. "I plan for how I will use money in the future."

NOT HEALTHY AT ALL   EXTREMELY HEALTHY

1   2   3   4   5   6   7   8   9   10

8. "I put time and effort into trying to save money."

NOT HEALTHY AT ALL   EXTREMELY HEALTHY

1   2   3   4   5   6   7   8   9   10

continued ⇒

9. "I understand and track my money."

1   2   3   4   5   6   7   8   9   10

10. "I find myself feeling like I don't have enough money."

1   2   3   4   5   6   7   8   9   10

Compare your answers. Where is there overlap and where do you differ? How would you like to handle those differences?

Your Long-Term Financial Goals

Each of you is coming to this marriage with dreams and goals for what your future will be like. When my husband and I got married, he dreamed of retiring early—something that had not even occurred to me at the time. Now, I'm on board with that goal for both of us. When you know where you are headed as a couple, making decisions in the present is much easier to do.

Whatever your dreams and financial goals, having a partner to share them with is a wonderful experience. Finances may have already come up in chapter 3, when we discussed your marriage goals. Take this opportunity to delve more deeply into why those financial goals are important to you. Given what you now know about your relationship with money, how do your long-term financial goals reflect that relationship?

To reach any future goal, you will need to shift and change your decisions because you are creating something new. Remember that slight detours or delays do not mean you won't get where you want to be. Patience, understanding, and grace will be required in this journey. There may also be times where one of you will have to step up in new ways. That's all okay and to be expected.

Knowing what each goal is and why it's so important to you will determine what the process of achieving that goal is like. The goal should not become more important than the relationship, or than valuing each other and treating each other with respect. As the Bible teaches, "What good is it for someone to gain the whole world, yet forfeit their soul?" (Mark 8:36). Goals are desires that should serve your marriage and bring you closer together.

 *Where Do You See Yourself?*

There are a number of ways to look at your financial goals. You can look at the income you'd like to make, the amount of money you have in savings or investments, or the amount of debt you have paid off. In the following exercise, you'll share your goals in each area. Complete the statements and then discuss with each other.

Partner A

IN THE NEXT YEAR:

I would like to be making _____(income or retirement goal).

I would like to have _____ in savings/investments.

I would like to have _____ debt.

This is important to me because _____

_____.

IN THE NEXT 5 YEARS:

I would like to be making _____ (income or retirement goal).

I would like to have _____ in savings/investments.

I would like to have _____ debt.

This is important to me because _____

_____.

IN THE NEXT 10 YEARS:

I would like to be making _____ (income or retirement goal).

continued ➡

I would like to have _____ in savings/investments.

I would like to have _____ debt.

This is important to me because _____

_____.

Partner B
IN THE NEXT YEAR:

I would like to be making _____ (income or retirement goal).

I would like to have _____ in savings/investments.

I would like to have _____ debt.

This is important to me because _____

_____.

IN THE NEXT 5 YEARS:

I would like to be making _____ (income or retirement goal).

I would like to have _____ in savings/investments.

I would like to have _____ debt.

This is important to me because _____

_____.

IN THE NEXT 10 YEARS:

I would like to be making _____ (income or retirement goal).

I would like to have _____ in savings/investments.

I would like to have _____ debt.

This is important to me because _____

_____ .

Your Current Financial Status

One of the most important things you can do as a couple is have honest conversations about money now. Any decisions you've made about money, good or bad, were influenced by a lot of factors. If you are proud of how you've used your money, celebrate that. If you are embarrassed or ashamed, offer yourself grace and understanding. Either way, your money decisions don't represent the totality of who you are as a person. Finances are just one aspect of your life that will be important to share as you and your partner join together to build a life.

It may be hard to have this conversation now, but it will be harder when you run into significant issues in managing money. If you are nervous about sharing your current financial status, take a moment to figure out why. This is important whether you have a lot of money or a little. Our society values money so much that we believe it determines our worth, but our value is found only in God: "For you know that it was not with perishable things such as silver or gold that you were redeemed from the empty way of life handed down to you from your ancestors, but with the precious blood of Christ, a lamb without blemish or defect" (1 Peter 1:18–19).

The right partner will not marry you because of how much money you have, or leave you based on what you lack. Your baseline—your understanding of where you start financially as a couple—is not the finish line. You have a lifetime to make money decisions that will support the life you want to have together. Total honesty here will only set you up for success later.

 *Find Your Baseline*

Fill in the following table to provide a framework for discussing your current financial status. Here, the goal is just to share the data and information; it's not necessary to do hours of research to find the exact figures. Just give your best estimate so you understand your financial position as a couple.

continued ➡

FINANCIAL INFORMATION
(use only those that apply)

	PARTNER A	PARTNER B
Annual salary		
Savings/investments		
Retirement		
Other liquid assets		
Monthly expenses		
Debt (credit card, student loan, mortgage, car, etc.)		
Other outstanding balances/ money owed		
Credit score		
Largest purchase in past 6 months		

After reviewing your answers, respond to the following prompts for further discussion.

1. How do you feel after sharing this information?

Partner A: _____

Partner B: _____

2. If you were giving a grade on how you and your partner are doing financially, what would it be?

Partner A: _____

Partner B: _____

3. What is one thing you think will work really well for you financially?

Partner A: _____

Partner B: _____

4. What is one thing that concerns you financially?

Partner A: _____

Partner B: _____

5. What would be a good next step to take in this area?

Partner A: _____

Partner B: _____

Managing Debt and Budgets

People have a lot of opinions on debt. Some debt is considered socially acceptable—for example, student loan debt or car debt—and some debt may be looked down on. Any debt you or your partner have is just the result of a financial choice that made sense at the time. From now on, you get to decide what is okay with you and what will be acceptable in your marriage.

If you and your partner have the same approach to managing money, this will be a breeze for you. If you have very different approaches, it's not cause for alarm. Conversations you have about managing debt and maintaining a budget should come from a place of giving each other the benefit of the doubt and wanting to understand any differences in opinion. Neither of you is right or wrong. When either one of you comes across as imposing your beliefs on the other, trust and safety in the relationship is compromised. If you are on opposite ends of the spectrum, take small steps to meet closer to the middle.

Live Within Your Means

The following exercise will help you start a conversation about how to handle debt and budgets in your marriage. For each of the following questions, select the most honest answers. In this discussion, create a safe space to candidly share your perspectives and expectations so you can appropriately problem-solve for any potential issues now.

1. I see debt as something that is:

PARTNER A
a. Not a big deal
b. Necessary for most couples
c. Bad, and should be avoided

PARTNER B
a. Not a big deal
b. Necessary for most couples
d. Bad, and should be avoided

2. I think any debt I bring:

PARTNER A
a. Is my responsibility only
b. Can be our joint responsibility
c. Can be paid by who makes the most

PARTNER B
a. Is my responsibility only
b. Can be our joint responsibility
c. Can be paid by who makes the most

3. I think any debt you bring should be:

PARTNER A
a. Your responsibility
b. Our joint responsibility
c. Paid by who makes the most

PARTNER B
a. Your responsibility
b. Our joint responsibility
c. Paid by who makes the most

4. Any new debt we incur together:

PARTNER A
a. Should be mutually agreed upon
b. Is our joint responsibility
c. Should be paid by who makes the most

PARTNER B
a. Should be mutually agreed upon
b. Is our joint responsibility
c. Should be paid by who makes the most

5. Budgeting for me is:

PARTNER A
a. Easy and fun
b. A necessary evil in life
c. Something I don't pay attention to

PARTNER B
a. Easy and fun
b. A necessary evil in life
c. Something I don't pay attention to

6. I would like for us to manage a budget by:

PARTNER A

a. Tracking and discussing our spending
b. Using cash as much as possible
c. Having monthly budget conversations

PARTNER B

a. Tracking and discussing our spending
b. Using cash as much as possible
c. Having monthly budget conversations

7. When we go over budget I'd like:

PARTNER A

a. To know why as soon as possible
b. To discuss where we will cut expenses
c. To adjust our budget so it's realistic

PARTNER B

a. To know why as soon as possible
b. To discuss where we will cut expenses
c. To adjust our budget so it's realistic

8. Any time there is an issue with the budget we will:

PARTNER A

a. Talk about where to cut expenses
b. Explore ways to make more money
c. Agree not to blame each other for errors

PARTNER B

a. Talk about where to cut expenses
b. Explore ways to make more money
c. Agree not to blame each other for errors

If this conversation uncovers significant differences, make a plan for what to do next. It's often helpful to look into a financial literacy program or meet with a financial planner.

If your differences come from diverging money philosophies, first identify where you already agree. Then determine whether you can still achieve your financial goals with different approaches. You may decide to try different things then evaluate.

If you find yourself at a complete impasse, seek the advice of a coach or counselor who can guide you to a workable resolution. Remember, as you seek Him first and put Him in charge of your goals, God will give you the perspective, wisdom, and insight to come together in this important area of your relationship.

TAKEAWAYS

Each of you brings different qualities and goals to your marriage, and how you handle money is part of that. The way you talk about money reflects your individual relationships with it. It's okay to have differing perspectives and approaches. Together you are creating a new financial blueprint that is realistic for you both.

Talk It Over

- What will work well about how you handle money together? Have any concerns come up?

- What next steps can you take to ensure you are managing financial decisions in a way that works for you as individuals?

- What attitudes did your family have toward money when you were growing up?

- What are you most proud of in how you have managed your money so far? What are you least proud of?

Keep in Mind

- Money is a topic that people have many strong opinions about. It's important to respect and try to understand your partner's views.

- Your relationship with money plays an important role in how you make financial decisions. Be aware of how it influences you and be willing to compromise.

- Your partner has their own relationship with money that may be different from yours. It's important to find ways to come together to meet your mutual financial goals. Communication and honesty are key.

Next Steps

- Identify one area where you can personally improve your relationship with money. Find a book or resource on this topic and apply what you learn.

- List three reasons why your financial goals are important. Discuss what achieving these goals will enable you to do.

- Create a list of ways to address the areas where you both have concerns about your current financial position.

CHAPTER 6

Work

Whatever you do, work at it with all your heart, as working for the Lord, not for human masters, since you know that you will receive an inheritance from the Lord as a reward. It is the Lord Christ you are serving.

COLOSSIANS 3:23-24

As humans on this planet, most of us will work to make a living and provide for our needs. We live in a world where hard work is applauded and accumulating wealth is desired. As a couple, you must find your own way with this topic. As discussed in chapter 5 (page 37), God is our ultimate provider. At the same time, He did design us to labor. Finding the balance—relying on the abundance of God while also working hard in our professions—is not always easy to do and may look different for each person.

In reading the preceding scripture, what stands out to me is the intention and purpose behind what we are doing. Some people are prone to overwork out of fear or low self-worth. Workaholism is a condition born from the need to achieve in order to feel valued. Workaholics view taking breaks as a sign of weakness or laziness. They devalue rest, even though God himself rested from His work and commanded us to do so as well.

Other people will toil and work themselves into the ground chasing things that don't truly matter or honor God. Even though God provides all we need, many are more concerned with showing their wealth and hard work through material possessions to gain the approval of others. Their overworking comes from insecurity or comparing themselves to others.

God wants you to find joy and fulfillment in the work you do, but work does not define you. Your position at your job does not make you better or worse than anyone else in God's eyes. How much money you earn has no bearing on who you are in this world. Your relationship with work should make your life better, not suck the life out of you.

How we view work is shaped by social norms and what we experienced growing up. If you grew up in a home with a parent who was preoccupied with work, that likely had a deep impact on you. As an adult, you may find yourself falling into the same patterns or partnering with someone who has the same work mentality.

As you think about the place for work in your life and marriage, consider it another way for you to honor God. Your work should not take away from your relationship with Him or with one another. It should not be a threat to your health or emotional well-being. No matter who your human boss or client is, you are working for God. You are advancing his vision for you. Think about where God wants to place you professionally and how He wants to use you. Is that reflected in your life right now? What things are potentially getting in the way? What changes are you willing to make to truly honor God and serve your marriage with the way that you work?

Our Career Goals

What are your professional goals? Where do you see yourself in your career in the next three to five years? Depending on your professional environment, this question may be an easy one to answer. In some industries, working for the next promotion, raise, or accolade is commonplace. High-achieving people thrive in this environment, and sometimes see their career as a proxy for their own worth.

God wants you to excel in your chosen career path, but never at the expense of your relationship. He does not want you to define yourself by your title, position, or salary. He wants you to find your worth in Him first. God loves you; your employer will never love you the way God loves you. He is the one who has given you the talents, skill set, and intelligence to contribute productively to your industry. Your success honors Him and what He has given you.

As you consider your careers as a couple, it's important to look at your goals from a few different perspectives. How will your family benefit from the time and energy required to achieve each goal? What might you have to sacrifice in the process? What will you need to give of yourself to achieve your goal? What is driving you to do so? Do those reasons represent who you want to be as an individual, partner, and/or parent?

If you find that one of you is very clear on your career goals while the other is not, think about how you can best support each other. This conversation might surface some work apathy or dissatisfaction. It's common for individuals to start out in a career and later find it is not their passion. Alternatively, one of you may be excelling in your career goals while the other is feeling overlooked or falling behind. Remember that you are now one as a couple. If one of you is rising professionally, it should benefit your family collectively. God will pour out His blessings in the way He sees fit, and in a way that serves His purpose. Even though you may carry out your career goals individually, they still serve your marriage overall.

Both Eyes on the Prize

In chapter 3, you may have briefly discussed your career goals as part of the larger conversation around marriage goals (page 22). This exercise will take that conversation deeper, helping you look at your internal and external motivations and come together to support each other in your respective journeys.

Partner A

A career goal I am working toward right now is_____.

This is important to me because _____.

When I achieve this goal, I will _____.

Achieving this goal will require _____.

I could really use my partner's help with _____.

Partner B

A career goal I am working toward right now is_____.

This is important to me because _____.

When I achieve this goal, I will _____.

Achieving this goal will require _____.

I could really use my partner's help with _____.

Now discuss steps each of you can take to support your partner's goals.

Achieving Work-Life Balance

In marriage, your partner wants to feel like they are a priority. Many things can take your attention and focus away from your relationship, and work is one of these. Most partners expect that work will occupy a certain amount of time, but when that time is exceeded, your marriage can feel out of balance.

This plays out most commonly when one partner works a lot more than the other. This issue intensifies when children enter the picture. The need for more time at home increases dramatically. At the same time, if one partner is the primary provider, their focus on fulfilling that financial role increases as well. The other partner is often left to take care of most of the child-rearing responsibilities, and if they are also working, this can become extremely overwhelming, leading to stress and tension in the relationship.

It is important to identify now what work-life balance will look like for you, especially if you have children or plan on having them. What feels like work-life balance for one person may not feel workable for the other. And because in most families it's necessary that one or both of you work, this can become an issue without an obvious solution.

If you anticipate this being an issue in your relationship (or if it is already), you need to find ways to protect your time together. Quality is more important than quantity. What aspects of spending time together are most important to you? Remember, it isn't your job to judge and condemn each other in this area. A lot of factors play into someone's ability to achieve a healthy work-life balance. It will also vary over time and with age. For now, focus on how to dedicate your time and attention to honor the type of partner you want to be and the value you place on your marriage.

What Work-Life Balance Means to You

The following exercise will help you define what work-life balance means to you and your family. Following is a checklist of items that might be included in your definition. Individually, rank each of these 12 items based on your priorities. Then discuss together the places where you had similar rankings. For items that are significantly different in your rankings, discuss options for striking a better balance that can work for you both.

Work-life balance means:

Partner A	Partner B	
		Not letting the stress of work negatively impact the way I show up at home.
		Maintaining boundaries for when I work and when I am present at home.
		Shutting my phone/email off and not responding to work requests outside of work hours.
		Declining optional work activities that conflict with home responsibilities.
		Checking in with each other first before committing to extra work activities.
		Inviting each other to work-related functions when significant others are allowed.
		Intentionally coming home early when work is light or my schedule allows.
		Intentionally taking days off for vacation or planned time together.
		Planning to rest and relax at home when I am under a lot of pressure.
		Not allowing my professional goals to conflict with my priorities at home.
		Creating time to connect with each other during the day, even while at work.
		Keeping the lines of communication open when we notice home is being neglected.

Dealing with a Job Loss or Transition

When you think about building your life together, it is most likely based on the here and now—where you work, what you do, and what your short-term career looks like. But as we all know, life can be unpredictable. You want to start thinking about how you might handle the unexpected.

Research shows that the average person will have twelve jobs in their lifetime (between the ages of eighteen and fifty-two) and have 5.8 stints of unemployment. It's likely that one or both of you will experience at least one major transition in your job status over time—more when you add in the transitions in and out of parental leave.

Job losses or transitions impact not only the family's finances, but in some cases the emotional health of the individual going through the change. A career or job is a part of one's identity, and to have an unexpected or undesired change can create confusion and impact self-esteem. People handle these transitions in many different ways.

Turning to God will be essential during this time. Seek His understanding as you navigate the transition. Ask Him to lead you and guide you in finding the next right opportunity. Trust Him to sustain you and provide you with all you need.

It's also important that you commit to supporting and understanding what your partner may be going through. There may be times when you can come together and honestly share your concerns, and times when it feels like discussing these issues is not helpful or productive on your own. I highly recommend you seek the help of a professional who can help you respond to this challenge in a unified way.

 *For Richer, For Poorer*

The following exercise will help you start the conversation about how you want to handle job losses and transitions in your marriage. For each of the following statements, indicate whether you agree or disagree. Discuss your responses with each other, sharing the rationale for your answers.

Partner A	Partner B	A = Agree D = Disagree:
		If either of us wants to leave our job, we will talk about it before any decision is made.
		If I am not performing well in my job, I will discuss it with my partner.
		If I am fearful of losing my job for any reason, I will have a conversation with my partner.
		If I lose my job, I will share that immediately with my partner.
		If I lose my job, and it's financially necessary, I will look for work right away.
		If I lose my job, and it's financially necessary, I will consider any job that I can start quickly.
		If I lose my job for any reason, I expect my partner to support me financially.
		If I lose my job for any reason, I expect my partner to be supportive and encouraging during the transition no matter what.
		If I am presented with an opportunity for a promotion or raise, I will discuss it with my partner before I make a decision.
		If I am presented with the opportunity to relocate or change jobs, I will discuss it with my partner before I make a decision.

After completing these questions, discuss what you noticed. Did your partner's answers surprise you? Why or why not?

TAKEAWAYS

In this chapter we covered the topic of work—your career goals, achieving work-life balance, and handling job loss and transitions. As individuals, you want to look at your own personal relationship with work and place it within the context of your marriage. We are driven to work for many different reasons. Ultimately, the work we do on this earth should honor God, and serve to enhance our families, not take away from them.

Talk It Over

- How has God spoken to you in this chapter?

- How have you been thinking about your relationship with your work/career?

- How would you rank work in your list of priorities right now? Are there shifts you are now committed to making?

- What drives you to work? What are you most motivated by?

- How can your relationship with work serve God and your relationship as a couple and not conflict with them?

Keep in Mind

- Your worth is never tied to your work—it comes from God. You are inherently worthy and valuable no matter what your title or position.

- It's good to have goals that come from a healthy place of honoring the skills, talents, and abilities God has given you.

- Work-life balance will look different for everyone. Be sure you are clear about the most important aspects for you as a couple.

Next Steps

- Identify three reasons you are motivated to work at the level that you do. Make sure you like your reasons and that you are achieving the balance you desire.

- List two boundaries you can set to ensure your time with your partner or family remains a priority.

- Once a month, set aside time to talk about work, including any issues, accomplishments, and changes.

CHAPTER 7

The Way We Communicate

> *May these words of my mouth and this meditation of my heart be pleasing in your sight, Lord, my Rock and my Redeemer.*
>
> **PSALM 19:14**

What if how we communicated with others was seen as an offering to the Lord? What would change if we were extremely aware that God was listening to our every word? Would He be pleased? Most of us have great moments of using our words in ways that please God, and other moments where we use our words in ways that grieve God. We are imperfect, in need of our perfect Savior to help guide us in this area.

I love the preceding scripture because it makes the connection between what comes out of your mouth and what's in your heart. The heart is the starting point for all communication. That's why we have this guidance from God: "Above all else, guard your heart, for everything you do flows from it" (Proverbs 4:23). This includes how you speak to others.

Our heart is the place where we carry the emotions of our thoughts. When we communicate, we are speaking from our feelings, whether they are happy, sad, frustrated, content, critical, or grateful. When thinking about the topic of communication in your marriage, you must also connect how you are feeling about yourself, each other, and your relationship.

No matter how you may be feeling, you want your words to be delivered with love, care, grace, and positive intention: "Let your conversation be always full of grace, seasoned with salt, so that you may know how to answer everyone" (Colossians 4:6). Strive for this even when you are feeling disappointed or upset. It's very easy to lose sight of this in the moment. When I am working with my clients, I help them come up with their own communication rules. These are the things they agree not to do or say, even when they are very angry with each other. What might be some rules you agree to in your own communication? How can keeping God in mind help you communicate well?

Many times, couples get stuck when communicating with each other because they become preoccupied with how their partner might react to what they say. Of course we all want to be emotionally intelligent and not intentionally say mean and hurtful things. I think it's also helpful to use God as a barometer for what you say and how you communicate. When you keep this psalm in mind, you will automatically speak in ways that honor your partner, even if you are communicating something difficult to hear.

Recognizing Our Communication Styles

When couples hit a bump in the road, communication issues are often the main problem. Maybe the couple has reached a point where each partner is not feeling heard or understood by the other, and their conversations have escalated to arguments and tense disagreements. In other instances, one person may feel like their partner is not communicating as openly and frequently as they should.

God designed each of us uniquely, and there is great value in the various ways we prefer to communicate. Still, it can be frustrating to experience communication breakdowns. We expect our partner to think the way we think and to speak as we would. But the way we communicate is a function of many factors: how our brains process information, our past experiences sharing our thoughts, our confidence in communicating effectively, and the comfort we feel with whom we are talking. It's important that you first be aware of your own communication style and preferences, and then begin to study your partner's, without judgment.

Commit to being open-minded about communication, and approach it with a heart of love and grace. Imagine if God were judging the way we communicate with Him! Instead, His ears are always open to us: "Then you will call on me and come and pray to me, and I will listen to you" (Jeremiah 29:12). It will serve you well to base your communication goals in listening, understanding, and sharing your experience without blaming the other person (in that order). Unnecessary arguments arise whenever one of these pieces is lost.

 How We Talk to Each Other

The following exercise will help you better understand your specific communication styles. Any differences that surface are wonderful opportunities for you to determine what will work best for your marriage.

For each of the items listed, indicate if this is mostly true or mostly false for you. Partner A can indicate their selection with a check mark and Partner B can use an asterisk.

Partner A   Partner B

Mostly True	Mostly False	Mostly True	Mostly False	
				I prefer to talk about any issues or concerns right away.
				I like to think things through before talking about them.
				I try to be careful in how I say things.
				I try to be honest in how I say things.
				I tend to focus more on how to solve the problem at hand.
				I tend to talk more about what's not working for me.
				It's easy for me to listen first before I respond.
				I like to talk first so I can have a clear mind to listen.
				I am more emotional when talking about sensitive issues.
				I am more rational when talking about sensitive issues.

As you look at your responses to the preceding items, discuss the following questions:

* What do you notice about your communication preferences?

* How do your current styles match up with how you imagine God would want you to communicate?

* What can you do to make sure your communication preferences and styles work well together?

Being Vulnerable

The secret to creating the deepest connection with your partner is being vulnerable. Vulnerability means opening yourself up, shedding your protective layers, and being available for unconditional love and acceptance. Being vulnerable feels risky at first, especially when you've had difficult experiences in the past with trusting and sharing. But there is always a lot to learn.

When you are vulnerable, you allow someone the opportunity to truly see you and love you at the highest level. Vulnerability first comes from your relationship with God. One psalmist declares, "Search me, God, and know my heart; test me and know my anxious thoughts" (Psalm 139:23). What is it like for you to invite God in to see all there is to see about you? He already does this, but when we consciously invite Him in, we welcome Him to truly become a part of us. We can do this because we know His love is never-ending, no matter what He might find.

You can have the same experience in your marriage when you allow yourself to be vulnerable. What might be getting in the way of you and your partner connecting and communicating with each other? Are there things about yourself you haven't shared for fear of rejection? Are there things you want to know about your partner that you haven't yet asked? Fear may be holding you back, but you can overcome this: "For the Spirit God gave us does not make us timid, but gives us power, love and self-discipline" (2 Timothy 1:7). Fear of being vulnerable causes us to focus on what we might be risking, but when you think about what you might gain and the depth of connection you can create, it's a risk worth taking.

 The Vulnerability Connection

The following exercise will help you explore your thoughts about vulnerability together and come to a greater understanding of what this will look like in your marriage. Vulnerability can grow over time as you experience more things together and become even more comfortable around each other.

Using the following prompts, share your thoughts with each other in a conversation. Partner A can answer all the questions first while Partner B listens, and then you will switch roles. When listening, your goal is to hear and understand, not necessarily to respond or react to what is shared.

1. Think about a time where you felt comfortable enough to be very vulnerable around your partner and share what created that comfort for you.

Partner A: _____

_____

_____

Partner B: _____

_____

_____

2. Describe a time when you noticed your partner being vulnerable with you and share how that moment impacted your relationship.

Partner A: _____

_____

_____

Partner B: _____

_____

_____

3. What makes it hard for you to be vulnerable with your partner?

Partner A: _____

_____

_____

Partner B: _____

_____

_____

continued ➡

4. How do you feel when your partner is vulnerable with you?

Partner A: _____

_____

_____

Partner B: _____

_____

_____

5. How would you describe vulnerability in your relationship right now?

Partner A: _____

_____

_____

Partner B: _____

_____

_____

After having this conversation, thank each other and express one thing you appreciated hearing. What did you learn about each other?

Making Adjustments

There will be times in your marriage when your communication is really working for you. You'll feel connected and comfortable, and operate like a highly functioning team. There will be other moments when you misunderstand each other, make incorrect assumptions, experience tension, and feel like you are headed in opposite directions. These moments can be frustrating, and it may seem hard to get back on track. But it is possible.

Your marriage will grow and evolve, just as you do as a couple. Your communication needs will also shift and change. Making adjustments is a process of continually assessing what's working, what's not working, and what needs to change. You want to always be asking the question, "What adjustments, if any, do we need to consider here?" For example, you might notice that you attempt to talk to your partner at certain times and they are distracted. To make an adjustment, you might share that you'd like to talk about something and ask them when it would be a good time.

Making adjustments is a fine-tuning, almost experimental process. You might try different ways of bringing issues to each other. For example, you might ask an open-ended question to see what your partner is thinking about the issue, or you might start out by sharing something you'd like to make better in your relationship. Focus on how quickly you can adjust, correct course, and recover when something isn't working.

God has already given us a template for how we should strive to communicate with each other: "Everyone should be quick to listen, slow to speak, and slow to become angry" (James 1:19). When considering what adjustments to make, you can always start with listening more, being more careful with your words, and managing your emotions well.

 ## *Communicate Intentionally*

What adjustments in your communication would be most pleasing to God? Use the following checklist to identify the areas where you'd like to improve *as a couple* in the way you communicate with each other. For each area you want to improve, place a check mark and discuss one specific thing you'd like to do differently. Feel free to write in any other adjustments you would like to make that are not listed here.

List of Communication Adjustments

_____ Address things that are bothering either one of us.

_____ Listen more to what the other person is saying.

_____ Pray before having a difficult conversation.

_____ Take more responsibility for our roles in an issue rather than blaming each other.

_____ Focus on how we can solve our problems and move forward.

_____ Create an environment where we feel comfortable sharing how we feel.

_____ Express more appreciation of each other.

_____ Refrain from judging each other's feelings or perspective.

_____ Be more careful with the tone we use when talking.

_____ Be more mindful of the timing when we have important conversations.

TAKEAWAYS

There is no couple that has perfect communication. Being open, honest, and vulnerable with each other from a place of love will help you connect with each other. It is this deep connection that makes communicating easier and more comfortable for everyone.

Talk It Over

- What have you learned about your partner's communication style? What stands out the most?

- What do you now appreciate about how you communicate as a couple?

- How do you see your different communication styles working together?

- What will you need to be intentional about in order to avoid misunderstanding each other?

- How will you acknowledge when you are doing really well with your communication?

- When you need help communicating more effectively, what resources can you access, or to whom can you go?

Keep in Mind

- You both have different communication styles and preferences that you will need to understand and make adjustments for.

- As you communicate with each other, make sure you are honoring God and using His principles to guide your conversations.

- You will have many opportunities to learn how to best communicate with each other; be willing to experiment and make adjustments, even if they feel uncomfortable at first.

Next Steps

- Pray beforehand whenever you need to have a difficult conversation.

- Think about one difference in your communication styles and identify one adjustment you will make to accommodate that difference.

- Identify a topic of conversation where you can allow yourself to be vulnerable. In the next week or so, initiate that conversation with your partner.

CHAPTER 8

Establishing Our Boundaries

You, my brothers and sisters, were called to be free. But do not use your freedom to indulge the flesh; rather, serve one another humbly in love. For the entire law is fulfilled in keeping this one command: "Love your neighbor as yourself."

GALATIANS 5:13–14

e are all individuals with free will. Any vow or promise you make to your partner is of your own accord. While you may enter a holy covenant, God gives you the choice to honor your commitment to each other. In this freedom, there is a responsibility to respect who you are and what you are creating in your union.

In this scripture from Galatians, we are instructed to use our freedom wisely; to not be led by our own fleshly desires, but to use our autonomy to serve each other with humility and love. For example, you might decide to make a sacrifice of your time to support your partner in some way. It's not something you have to do, but you *choose* it as an act of service and love. When both of you are doing this at your full capacity, your marriage will be incredibly fulfilling. You will create safety, connection, intimacy, excitement, and love. It will be easier to operate with integrity and righteousness.

While this is the ideal, it can sometimes be hard to fully define what it means to "indulge in the flesh." One person might draw the line at yelling in anger; another might draw the line at going against an established agreement. As we've discussed in previous chapters, we all come with unique experiences, ideas, and perspectives that shape what we expect and will tolerate in a relationship. As we begin to explore the topic of boundaries, this will be important to keep in mind.

In the preceding scripture, the Apostle Paul offers us a shortcut in discerning what is appropriate or inappropriate in various circumstances. Loving your neighbor—in this case, your partner—as yourself means you are consciously assessing if you are operating in the same manner that you would want them to. In a marriage, this takes many forms. One of the most obvious is related to fidelity, but also important are boundaries related to finances, parenting, extended family, and work. For instance, you may expect your partner to be up-front about financial decisions they've made or disciplinary actions they've taken with children. If it's something you would like to know or make decisions about, you should offer the same consideration to your partner.

Being able to love each other as you love yourselves requires first that you honor, respect, and uphold yourselves to certain standards. God is always teaching us how to operate at our full potential. When you are focused on living at that level, adhering to any boundaries that support your marriage becomes a way of life.

The scripture from Galatians reminds us that we are called to be free. We have power over any thought, feeling, or action that would violate a sacred vow or boundary in our marriage. In Romans, Paul reminds us, "For sin shall no longer be your master, because you are not under the law, but under grace" (Romans 6:14). By God's grace and the Holy Spirit within us, establishing and maintaining appropriate boundaries in marriage is something we are already equipped to do.

It's All About Trust

Trust. We hear so much about this topic. How it's earned. How it's lost. Who deserves it. Each of you will enter this marriage with different ideas of what trust means in your relationship. This is also an area greatly informed by past experiences, both outside of your relationship and within it.

It's important for you as a couple to come up with your own common understanding of trust, and how building and maintaining trust will support the kind of marriage you want to have. Knowing what you personally need in order to trust, as well as what you are committed to doing to demonstrate your trustworthiness, is essential. These are conversations many couples don't have until trust has been violated in some way.

Having a conversation about trust before a betrayal will help you create a strong foundation of understanding and realistic expectations without the emotional intensity that can make these conversations difficult. A great place to start is examining your relationship with God. Is God someone you've decided to trust? Why or why not? How do you handle things when you have a hard time trusting God? How does it feel to truly trust God when you do? Your thoughts about trusting God will influence the way you trust other people in your life.

Trusting someone else is also built on your ability to trust yourself. When you are secure and grounded in who you are, it can be easier to trust your partner because their words or actions don't diminish your identity. People who have trust issues may have been betrayed in the past, but it's also critical that they acknowledge and heal the ways they may have betrayed themselves by not placing appropriate boundaries or speaking up when they felt wronged. When it comes to issues of trust, invite God into your heart through prayer so that you might forgive, and release any pain you might be holding on to.

 ## Staying Trustworthy

The following exercise will help you discuss your unique perspectives on the topic of trust and define what trust will look like in your marriage.

Complete the following sentence prompts on your own and share your responses with each other.

1. Trust in a marriage is earned by:

Partner A: _____

Partner B: _____

2. Trust in a marriage is lost by:

Partner A: _____

Partner B: _____

3. Trust in a marriage can be rebuilt when:

Partner A: _____

Partner B: _____

4. My ability to trust you is determined by:

Partner A: _____

Partner B: _____

continued ➡

5. I demonstrate that I am trustworthy by:

Partner A: _____

Partner B: _____

6. I find it hard to trust anyone when:

Partner A: _____

Partner B: _____

7. If you make a mistake or betray my trust, I will need:

Partner A: _____

Partner B: _____

After sharing your responses, discuss what each of you can do to deepen the trust in your relationship.

Boundaries Between Us

Boundaries exist to keep you safe emotionally, physically, and spiritually. Boundaries also define when a line has been crossed. Boundaries are rules and decisions you enforce to protect yourself. They are not ultimatums. They are not intended to control or manipulate the other person. Boundaries can be empowering and helpful as you determine what is and isn't acceptable to you, both individually and as a couple.

When couples do have conversations about boundaries, it usually relates to interactions with people outside of the marriage. But you have a wonderful opportunity to first think about boundaries *within* your marriage. Boundaries can relate to conversations you have, language that is used, requests that are made, how you talk to each other, how you physically interact with each other, how you manage certain aspects of your life (finances, parenting, etc.), things you share, and roles you assume.

Boundaries work best when you are clear on the values and principles upon which they are based. God's Word is a great reference point for standards of behavior (e.g., how you speak to and treat each other), which can be important in determining boundaries. It is also important that you determine what your next steps will be should a boundary be violated. *What will I do to protect myself?* is the key question, not *What must my partner do?* We can never control the actions of others, only our own responses. If an argument escalates and your partner starts yelling, but that's a boundary for you, what will you do for *you*? Will you exit the room and end the conversation? If your partner makes a financial decision that crosses a boundary for you, will you open a separate bank account or start saving money yourself?

Many couples operate on a model of blame and consequences. I encourage you to allow God to convict your partner if they have done something wrong, and to focus on how you can work through and heal the impact of their words or actions. This might look like being kind and loving to yourself, deciding to forgive and release any resentment, and focusing on how you can move forward. Boundaries do not need to be enforced from a place of anger or bitterness. Instead, they can be viewed as a gracious act of love for yourself and honor for your partner.

 ## *Set Your Boundaries*

Together, use the following topic areas to create your own boundaries as a couple. Feel free to add additional topic areas that are relevant to your relationship.

TOPIC AREA	WHAT IS NOT ACCEPTABLE	WHAT IS ACCEPTABLE
Things we talk about openly		
Language or words we use		
How we express anger		
Things we can request of each other		
How we touch each other		
How we manage money		
How we parent our children		
How we connect during the day		

Boundaries with Others

People are often fully aware of when they cross a boundary with another person. Sexual infidelity, divulging information shared with you in confidence, or telling lies would for the most part be considered crossing boundaries. Most traditional marriage vows include the line "forsaking all others." This means keeping your spouse at a more heightened level of importance, intimacy, and connection than any other person.

It is often the gray areas that couples wrestle with. These are things like flirting—in person or over text messages—or spending time with someone in a questionable social setting, sharing a sensitive conversation with someone, or downplaying an interaction with someone else. Often these boundaries aren't discussed until after something becomes an issue. You want to be having those conversations now.

Equally as common are boundaries related to extended family. One of you may prefer daily phone conversations with a sibling and weekly dinners at Mom's, while the other would rather visit family less frequently. This can be an extremely touchy topic, and although God has instructed us to "leave and cleave," interpretations of what this actually means will vary.

The key when it comes to boundaries with others is to keep the lines of communication open and make no assumptions. What seems okay to one person might be undesirable to another. When you can approach these conversations with a mind to understand and relate to where your partner is coming from, it will be easier to find a middle ground.

 What's Okay and What's Not Okay

The following exercise will help you start a conversation about boundaries with others. For each of the following statements, indicate your level of agreement. Partner A will select their answer by circling the appropriate number, and Partner B will select their answer by placing an asterisk by the appropriate number. Discuss why you gave the response that you did in order to deepen your understanding of each other.

1. It is okay to flirt with someone in person or via text as long as it doesn't lead to something more.

   STRONGLY DISAGREE   STRONGLY AGREE
   1   2   3   4   5   6   7   8   9   10

2. A person should tell their partner if someone else expresses romantic or sexual interest in them.

   STRONGLY DISAGREE   STRONGLY AGREE
   1   2   3   4   5   6   7   8   9   10

3. If a person is unfaithful in any way (emotionally or physically), they should tell their partner right away.

STRONGLY DISAGREE   STRONGLY AGREE

1   2   3   4   5   6   7   8   9   10

4. It's okay to treat a coworker to lunch.

STRONGLY DISAGREE   STRONGLY AGREE

1   2   3   4   5   6   7   8   9   10

5. It's okay to share intimate details of our relationship with others that are trustworthy.

STRONGLY DISAGREE   STRONGLY AGREE

1   2   3   4   5   6   7   8   9   10

6. If a family member needs my help, it's okay to cancel plans we may have together.

STRONGLY DISAGREE   STRONGLY AGREE

1   2   3   4   5   6   7   8   9   10

7. Family and close friends are always welcome in our home without needing to check with each other.

STRONGLY DISAGREE   STRONGLY AGREE

1   2   3   4   5   6   7   8   9   10

8. It's okay to independently spend as much time as we'd like with friends and family.

STRONGLY DISAGREE   STRONGLY AGREE

1   2   3   4   5   6   7   8   9   10

9. It's okay for my partner to see who I am friends with on social media.

STRONGLY DISAGREE   STRONGLY AGREE

1   2   3   4   5   6   7   8   9   10

10. It's okay for my partner to have access to passwords on my phone, computer, or other device.

STRONGLY DISAGREE   STRONGLY AGREE

1   2   3   4   5   6   7   8   9   10

After sharing your answers, discuss the following questions:

- How are you feeling about your individual perspectives on boundaries?

- How is having this discussion now helpful to you moving forward?

If there are significant points of disagreements, it may be helpful to reach out for additional support from a trusted mentor or marriage professional.

When Boundaries Are Crossed

Boundaries are not intended to control how your partner behaves. That would be an impossible task! Instead, you should discuss now what steps you could take individually and as a couple when a boundary is crossed. For example, if there is infidelity in your marriage, you might decide as an individual that you will hold off on being intimate with your partner and then collectively seek professional help to address what led to the infidelity.

When boundaries are crossed, it triggers trust issues. The person who was offended begins to question if they are emotionally, physically, or spiritually safe. During these times, it's more important than ever to press into a deeper relationship with God. He will never betray your trust. When you can fill yourself up with His love and grace, determining what to do in your marriage will be clearer.

When boundaries are crossed in a marriage, one or both people are left wounded. For our own sakes, we want to be quick to forgive, but it does not mean we have to condone or continue to allow unacceptable behavior or treatment.

Knowing exactly what you want to do if a boundary is crossed is a continually evolving process. Your responses may change over time, but you probably already know your deal-breakers and when you might choose to spend time apart for physical or emotional safety. Share that with your partner. This is a great opportunity to have an open and honest conversation.

 *Make a Game Plan*

Following is a list of potential boundaries that might get crossed in a marriage. For each, complete the sentence with what you would do and how you would like to come together as a couple to address the issues.

Example: My partner has been emotionally unfaithful (spending extra time or having intimate conversations with someone else).

Partner A: I would ask to have a conversation with them and the other person.

Partner B: I would demand that all communication with this other person stops.

Together we agree to check in regularly about what's happening and how the unfaithful partner will maintain appropriate boundaries.

1. My partner has been emotionally unfaithful (spending extra time or having intimate conversations with someone else).

Partner A: I would_____

Partner B: I would_____

Together we agree to _____

2. My partner has been sexually unfaithful.

Partner A: I would_____

Partner B: I would_____

Together we agree to _____

3. My partner yells in anger during an argument.

Partner A: I would_____

Partner B: I would_____

Together we agree to _____

4. My partner makes a large purchase without discussing it with me first.

Partner A: I would_____

Partner B: I would_____

Together we agree to _____

continued ➡

5. My partner does not adhere to our established budget.

Partner A: I would _____

Partner B: I would _____

Together we agree to _____

6. My partner does not follow through on something they agreed to do.

Partner A: I would _____

Partner B: I would _____

Together we agree to _____

7. My partner does something that I consider unsafe or harmful.

Partner A: I would _____

Partner B: I would _____

Together we agree to _____

TAKEAWAYS

Boundaries are important in a marriage. While we all have free will, it is important that we honor God, ourselves, and our partner by how we choose to conduct ourselves. You'll continue to have these important conversations over time as various situations arise. You will be served by seeking God's wisdom in determining what will be best for your marriage.

Talk It Over

- What was most important to you from this chapter?

- What concerns came up for you about how to set and maintain boundaries? What challenges have you had in the past?

- Where are you both already in agreement about certain boundaries? How has that made your relationship easier?

- What else do you want your partner to know about boundaries and trust?

- What is the most important boundary you want to focus on as a couple?

Keep in Mind

- It's important to be proactive and have discussions now about boundaries, rather than waiting until an issue presents itself.

- At some point in most relationships, a boundary is crossed; when this happens, focus on protecting yourself while still respecting your partner.

Next Steps

- As you create your boundaries, find scripture that supports your ideas, and ask God to help you maintain the boundaries.

- Review the boundaries you created in this chapter. How can you trust that you and your partner will maintain each boundary?

- Identify your most important boundaries in a marriage and why they are so important to you.

CHAPTER 9

Dealing with Conflict

> *A gentle answer turns away wrath, but a harsh word stirs up anger.*
>
> PROVERBS 15:1

n every relationship there will be differing perspectives and times when you do not agree. The goal is not to always get along, but to effectively navigate points of conflict in ways that help you grow and become stronger as a couple. In Proverbs 15:1, God gives us a blueprint for how to handle conflict: to be gentle. Ironically, this is the opposite of how we feel when we are upset and angry.

Our God is so wise, and He knows what works best. I want you to think of a time when you were angry with someone and they met you with harsh or critical words. It's likely that their response only fueled your anger and did not help the situation. Now, think of a time when you were angry and someone acknowledged how you felt, expressed empathy, or gave you an apology. You were probably more likely to calm down and resolve what was happening for you.

I love this scripture because this is how our Heavenly Father approaches us when we make mistakes and miss the mark. He does not condemn us and make us feel even worse. Instead, "he is faithful and just and will forgive us our sins and purify us from all unrighteousness" (1 John 1:9). Take a moment to think about the peace that comes from God's grace and mercy. How much more inspired are we to do better when we receive love, as opposed to being condemned?

In your marriage, you want to resolve your conflict while maintaining an intimate connection with each other. There will be times when you misunderstand each other, judge each other, or offend through your words or actions. At the same time, you have the power to respond with gentleness and grace. Ephesians 4:26 instructs us, "in your anger do not sin." No matter how you are feeling, you have a choice in how you respond. You are responsible for those choices.

In heightened moments of conflict, it's hard to respond with gentleness. When you have trouble in this area, seek the help of the Holy Spirit. God promises to give us help in Ezekiel 36:27: "And I will put my Spirit in you and move you to follow my decrees and be careful to keep my laws." God does not ask us to do anything He has not already given us the power to do. I believe our most valuable conflict resolution tool is the attitude with which we communicate. When your hearts are softened toward each other and your words are seasoned with salt (Colossians 4:6), you will be able to talk through your issues successfully and resolve your conflicts with a greater understanding and appreciation of each other.

Managing Triggers

Having triggers is part of being human. Triggers can include feeling extremely frustrated when your partner is late, getting very angry when they don't respond to your questions, or becoming resentful when they don't follow through on an agreement. Experiencing triggers in your marriage does not mean something is wrong or that your marriage won't be successful. But mismanaging triggers can create distance and breakdowns in a relationship.

Most people I encounter respond to triggers by blaming their partner. When something upsetting happens, they are quick to point it out and want their partner to "correct" that behavior or way of thinking. Resolving the trigger becomes the responsibility of the "wrong" partner. The problem with this way of operating is that one person is trying to control the other and it keeps the triggered partner from ever understanding *why* they are triggered in the first place.

A better approach to managing triggers is to consider them an opening for your own self-awareness and personal growth. Most triggers are not about what is happening in the moment but are the accumulation of similar incidents over time, often originating from childhood. They represent unhealed wounds that, when surfaced in marriage, can create intense reactions. When you can first consider why you are having such an intense reaction to a situation, you can identify the places where you might still need healing and transformation. God is showing you where you still need His perspective and guidance.

What Sets You Off?

The following exercise will help you uncover some of your top triggers and prepare you both to approach these sensitive situations with greater understanding and compassion. It will keep you from blaming each other for how you feel and instead position you to use these moments as opportunities to create a deeper and more intimate connection to each other.

   Complete the following sentences individually. Take the time you need to come up with your honest answers. Then share your answers with each other. When sharing, the goal is to listen to what your partner is saying and not to offer your thoughts about how they should handle triggers. This is a time to learn and understand important information about each other.

1.   A type of situation I have trouble managing is:

Partner A: _____

Partner B: _____

2.   My immediate reaction is:

Partner A: _____

Partner B: _____

3.   This is because I feel:

Partner A: _____

Partner B: _____

4.   I feel this way because it reminds me of:

Partner A: _____

Partner B: _____

continued ➡

5. When this happens the best thing for us to do is:

Partner A: _____

Partner B: _____

Understanding and managing your triggers is something that may be best supported with the help of a professional. If you have many triggers in your relationship, a deep dive into the source of your feelings may be beneficial.

Handling Conflict

When thinking of conflict in a relationship, most people think of confrontation or heated arguments. But constructive conflict can teach you valuable lessons about yourselves and one another. Conflict is just two people who have different thoughts, ideas, and opinions coming together to discuss. Like so many of the other topics we've covered (e.g., money), conflict in and of itself is neutral, but how it is handled in a relationship matters greatly.

Sometimes couples are on opposite ends of the spectrum when it comes to conflict. One person may be more conflict-avoidant, while the other may prefer to surface any potential problems in their mind. Like so many things, God has instructed us on how to handle our differences. The guiding scripture I like to use when thinking about confrontation is about "speaking the truth in love" (Ephesians 4:15). Conflict does not have to feel like aggression or anger. It can look like two people who respect and honor each other coming together to talk about hard things they may not see eye to eye on.

This perspective will change everything about the way you handle problems in your marriage. Even when you strongly disagree and are totally opposed to what your spouse is saying or doing, you do not have to resort to hostile comments and destructive responses. How you handle conflict in these early stages of your relationship will set the foundation for future problem-solving. When bringing issues to each other, seek God's wisdom and be clear about your intent.

Speaking Truth in Love

The following exercise will help you discuss how you want to handle conflict in your marriage. Part of what will help you effectively navigate any challenges is having an awareness of when anger and frustration are leading you more than grace and love.

For each of the following items listed, check off the preferences that are most true for you and discuss together why you selected your answers.

CONFLICT PREFERENCES	PARTNER A	PARTNER B
When you are angry, I prefer you approach me immediately, even if you are still upset.		
When you are angry, I prefer you take time to calm down before you approach me.		
When we disagree, I prefer to share my point first and then hear yours.		
When we disagree, I prefer to hear your thoughts first, and then share mine.		
If I say something that offends you, I want you to give me specific examples.		
If I say something that offends you, I need the chance to explain myself.		

continued ➡

CONFLICT PREFERENCES	PARTNER A	PARTNER B
If we have an argument that gets too intense, I will likely shut down and walk away.		
If we have an argument that gets too intense, I will want to keep talking until we can both calm down.		

Taking a big picture look at each of your respective preferences, what do you notice? How will this help you as a couple? What things might you need to pay closer attention to moving forward?

When Communication Breaks Down

Communication breakdowns happen in every marriage. Someone will say something the wrong way, or something will be interpreted the wrong way. The book of James is a great resource for seeking God's wisdom in this area; it even acknowledges that we will not be perfect: "We all stumble in many ways. Anyone who is never at fault in what they say is perfect, able to keep their whole body in check" (James 3:2). The more you approach communication breakdowns as inevitable, and as opportunities to learn and improve, the better your communication will be.

Communication breakdowns don't mean something is going horribly wrong in your marriage. Communication, like any skill, is something you get better at with time. You are two people who have had different experiences with how you were communicated with growing up. That exposure plays a large role in how you communicate as adults.

The goal in addressing communication breakdowns is to focus on how you want to communicate with each other and to be willing to make adjustments. Some individuals will enter a marriage with the limiting belief that they are not good at communicating, when in fact they can learn to open up. Others may enter the marriage thinking they are great communicators, only to learn that they are not great listeners—which is equally as important, if not more so, than expressing oneself.

The Bible helps us understand God's standards for handling communication issues. In Ephesians 4:29, we are instructed, "Do not let any unwholesome talk come out of your mouths, but only what is helpful for building others up according to their needs, that it may benefit those who listen." Even in your misunderstandings, you can encourage each other and work together to improve your communication.

Your Communication Breakdown Plan

Communication breakdowns can be resolved when you focus on working together. The following exercise will help you to determine how best to work together and learn from any disagreements, misunderstandings, or mistakes in your communication. Together as a couple, create your own Communication Breakdown Plan. Complete your answers for each of the following scenarios.

1. When we have breakdowns in our communication, we will:

_____

_____

2. When one of us is primarily at fault for a breakdown, the other person agrees to:

_____

_____

3. We can work to prevent unnecessary communication breakdowns by:

_____

_____

4. When we have communication breakdowns we can use them as opportunities to grow by:

_____

_____

5. When we notice we are having the same recurring communication breakdowns we will:

_____

_____

continued ➡

Apologies and Forgiveness

For some people, apologizing is easy; for others, it is very hard. If you are quick to apologize and forgive, see it as a gift. God deeply values when we admit our wrongs and forgive each other, yet, in some instances, this is extremely hard to do.

Couples get stuck on this topic when they look to each other instead of looking to God. People may try to determine whether someone "deserves" an apology or forgiveness rather than recognizing that we have already been commanded by our Heavenly Father to make amends. Apologies and forgiveness should not be based on merit, but on obedience to God. We are to be "kind and compassionate to one another, forgiving each other, just as in Christ God forgave you" (Ephesians 4:32).

When you can apologize, you live free. You are not burdened by your mistakes, and you open the door to a greater connection. Apologizing doesn't mean you always have to take the blame. You can apologize for any wrongdoing on your part, or express regret that your partner is feeling negatively about a situation. There are times where you will want to apologize even without fully understanding the details of an encounter in an effort to connect with what your partner is going through.

We must also remember that Christ paid the price for everyone's sin. This includes the sin of your partner. It may seem necessary to hold onto your hurt and anger, especially if no apology is forthcoming, but when we lean on the sacrifice of our Savior, instant healing is available to us. If there is anything that will support your marriage becoming a success, it's committing to a regular practice of apologizing and forgiving.

 Forgiving as Christ Forgave

The following exercise will help you uncover how comfortable you are with apologizing and forgiveness in your relationship. For each of the following items, indicate the degree to which you agree when it comes to offering an apology or forgiveness. Partner A should indicate their response by circling the appropriate number. Partner B should indicate their response by placing an asterisk by the appropriate number. As you rate your answers for each question, discuss why you gave the answer you did.

1. It's easy for me to apologize when I know I am wrong.

    STRONGLY DISAGREE   STRONGLY AGREE
    1   2   3   4   5   6   7   8   9   10

2. It's easy for me to apologize, even if the other person is angry or confrontational.

    STRONGLY DISAGREE   STRONGLY AGREE
    1   2   3   4   5   6   7   8   9   10

3. It's easy for me to apologize even if the other person is also in the wrong.

STRONGLY DISAGREE   STRONGLY AGREE

1   2   3   4   5   6   7   8   9   10

4. It's easy for me to apologize even when I think the other person won't accept my apology.

STRONGLY DISAGREE   STRONGLY AGREE

1   2   3   4   5   6   7   8   9   10

5. It's easy for me to apologize for both big and small offenses.

STRONGLY DISAGREE   STRONGLY AGREE

1   2   3   4   5   6   7   8   9   10

6. It's easy for me to forgive small things that happen more than one time.

STRONGLY DISAGREE   STRONGLY AGREE

1   2   3   4   5   6   7   8   9   10

7. It's easy for me to forgive even if the other person doesn't apologize.

STRONGLY DISAGREE   STRONGLY AGREE

1   2   3   4   5   6   7   8   9   10

8. I see forgiveness as something that helps me feel better.

STRONGLY DISAGREE   STRONGLY AGREE

1   2   3   4   5   6   7   8   9   10

9. I find it easy to forgive most things when someone apologizes.

STRONGLY DISAGREE   STRONGLY AGREE

1   2   3   4   5   6   7   8   9   10

10. It's easy for me to forgive even if I'm really hurt by someone else's actions.

STRONGLY DISAGREE   STRONGLY AGREE

1   2   3   4   5   6   7   8   9   10

TAKEAWAYS

Conflict will happen in a marriage, and the way you speak to each other and work together to recover from arguments is so important. Relying on God's instruction in this area paves the way to handle your issues productively and from a place of love.

Talk It Over

- What have you discovered about your ability to apologize and forgive? What have you learned about your partner's?

- How did people communicate with you growing up? How do you think that affects the way you communicate as an adult?

- In what ways have you handled conflict well in the past? Where are the places that you get stuck as a couple when you don't agree?

- How can keeping God in the midst of your relationship help you navigate conflict well?

- Where might you need His help the most?

Keep in Mind

- Conflict in your marriage can create greater understanding and help your relationship become stronger.

- You came together to love each other and treat each other well. Approach disagreements with love, grace, and kindness.

- God has offered us guidance on how to talk to each other and how to address offenses, and seeking His Word will always put you on the right path.

Next Steps

- Whenever your differences are creating distance, pray that God would give you understanding, perspective, and insight as to how best to approach your partner in a loving and kind way.

- Whenever you have a communication breakdown, assess what happened and identify one thing you could have done better to make for a more productive conversation.

- Make apologizing a habit in your relationship by generously offering your apology and genuinely caring about how your partner feels.

CHAPTER 10

Family and Friends

> *The man said, "This is now bone of my bones and flesh of my flesh; she*
> *shall be called 'woman,' for she was taken out of man." That is why a man leaves*
> *his father and mother and is united to his wife, and they become one flesh.*
>
> GENESIS 2:23–24

In marriage, you are uniting with your partner to create anew. Your old life cannot compete with the new life you are building together. This popular scripture from Genesis offers this concept of leaving and cleaving. Like anything God instructs us to do, the benefits always outweigh the risks.

The creation of Eve signifies a oneness with Adam. God could have created her from another pile of dust, but He intentionally chose to create her *from* man. Part of Adam was sacrificed to give to Eve so that she could be created. For some, leaving their family of origin is a huge sacrifice. Entering into a lifelong covenant with someone you haven't known nearly as long can feel like uncharted territory. As humans, we are attracted to what's familiar. Our families represent the foundation of the identity we've come to know, as we were constantly being shaped by our home environments.

Uniting together and becoming one in your new marital family offers equal influence to both partners. Without this understanding, as described in the preceding scripture, one partner might impose their family norms on the other without regard for their preferences. When you operate in oneness, there is less room for "my way" or "your way," but there is a wonderful opportunity to create "our way."

This scripture also shows us how to prioritize our marriage. When we are single, our primary family might have the bulk of our time, attention, and effort. Yet, when we marry, the marriage takes precedence. This in no way means you are to completely disregard your family, but when you have competing priorities and don't know what to do, this guidance prevails.

I want to emphasize how important and difficult this can be in certain circumstances. Our families have an enormous pull on our hearts and emotions. Many decisions that are made concerning family come from love and a sense of duty. Your individual family dynamics and the dynamics in your marriage should support and serve each other. As partners, you want to support a healthy relationship with family and not do anything to create division.

The relationship with your extended family should enhance your marriage and vice versa. When one is taking away from the other, something is out of order. It is God's intention that your family be whole and healthy, and this includes your immediate and extended family. Psalm 133:1 says, "How good and pleasant it is when God's people live together in unity!"

If you find yourself struggling in this area, ask God to give you wisdom and insight. Seek clarity on whether the issues are arising from poor prioritization or if one of you might be struggling with jealousy. Understanding what's acceptable and when boundaries are crossed is very important. This chapter will help you do just that.

Our Family and Our Relationship

Marriage is the bringing together of two families. In some partnerships, the families look and operate much the same way. For example, both families may enjoy celebrating holidays and vacations together or share similar religious beliefs. Partners are often drawn to these similarities in their upbringing and expect many of the same patterns as they build their own family.

In other partnerships, the families might look very different. One person may have grown up in a two-parent home, while another may have grown up in a single-parent home or been raised by other relatives. There may be differences in the amount of time spent with family and in the level of closeness. They may also have different ways of handling conflict. Individuals may be drawn to these differences, as one family may represent the things they longed for in their own.

Your respective upbringings will help you understand each other, as you determine how you would like your *own* family to operate. This is an important area in which to be open, honest, and flexible with each other.

Individuals in a couple often fall into the trap of expecting their partner to agree to things just because it's the way things were done in their family. You'll need to assess what is true for the both of you, regardless of the expectations or norms set forth by your respective families. This is an area to seek God's wisdom and guidance, as He provides the model for how families should function at their highest capacity.

 *A New Family History*

The following exercise will help you to uncover similarities and differences between your families of origin. You will also have the opportunity to decide which aspects of your upbringing you'd like to keep and integrate into your new family. Feel free to add additional family elements that are not listed.

Partner A

FAMILY ELEMENT	HOW THIS WAS HANDLED IN MY FAMILY
Conflict	
Financial decisions	
Mealtime	
Activities/vacations	
Daily conversation	
Work	
Household responsibilities	
Childcare	
Time with extended family	
Time with friends	
Alone time	

Partner B

FAMILY ELEMENT	HOW THIS WAS HANDLED IN MY FAMILY
Conflict	
Financial decisions	
Mealtime	
Activities/vacations	
Daily conversation	
Work	
Household responsibilities	
Childcare	
Time with extended family	
Time with friends	
Alone time	

Our Family

FAMILY ELEMENT	HOW WE'D LIKE TO HANDLE IT IN OUR FAMILY
Conflict	
Financial decisions	
Mealtime	
Activities/vacations	
Daily conversation	
Work	
Household responsibilities	
Childcare	
Time with extended family	
Time with friends	
Alone time	

Our Friends and Our Relationship

The company you keep matters. The qualities you look for in your friends as a single person might change once you are married, and those might change again once you have children. As you enter into marriage, it's important that your friends play a positive role in the new life you are creating. Many marriages are ruined when one or both partners prioritize their friends over one another or spend a lot of time with friends who don't value the covenant of marriage. The Bible talks about how "bad company corrupts good character" (1 Corinthians 15:33).

When you marry, you join together your lives—including parts of your social lives. You want to strike the balance of having your own friends and friends that you see as a couple. It's important to talk through your expectations for how much time you spend with your respective friends and how you want to handle friendships that your partner may not approve of. These types of discussions are important as you build trust and demonstrate that your marital relationship is a priority. It can sometimes be difficult to put your marriage above other long-term friendships, but when you keep in mind the future you are building with your partner, it will be easier to put close friendships in their proper place.

It is essential in a healthy marriage for both partners to have trusted friends with whom they can share important parts of their lives. There will be seasons in your marriage where your spouse will meet your needs for meaningful connection, and other times where a close circle of friends may be just what you need. Your friendships can help support you through the ups and downs of marriage. One of the greatest things you can do for your marriage is to ask God to send you godly friends who will pray with and for your marriage, and offer godly advice when you need it.

 Cultivating Godly Friendships

The following exercise will help you get to know each other's preferences and expectations when it comes to time spent with friends. For each of the following items, indicate if you agree that it's acceptable and okay (A), or if you find it unacceptable and disapprove (D). For any items where your answers differ, decide how you will come to a resolution. Write your expectations and resolutions on the lines.

Partner A   Partner B

Partner A	Partner B	
		It's okay to go out alone with friends who are not married.
		It's okay to hang out alone with opposite sex friends.
		It's okay to talk with certain friends about issues in our marriage.
		It's okay to vacation with friends without each other.
		It's okay to cancel our plans together if a friend is in need.
		It's okay to have friends stop by without advance notice.
		It's okay for me to have friends my partner does not like.

Expectations and agreements that surfaced during this conversation:

_____

_____

_____

_____

Holidays and Traditions

You're both bringing to your marriage your own ideas about how holidays and traditions should be handled. One of you may like big celebrations, while the other may prefer a more understated acknowledgment of holidays. Maybe both your families have similar holiday schedules, and you have to figure out how to split the time. No one approach is better than the other. You have the opportunity to decide how you will make it work.

Each of you should consider a few things. You want to understand why celebrating a holiday in a particular way, or not at all, is important to you. Think beyond "that's how it was done when I was growing up" and really identify why it's important to you now. Determine which holidays and traditions are more meaningful for you than others, and when you prefer to gather with extended family or just celebrate together. Consider whether there are times when you would be willing to celebrate holidays separately, especially if travel is involved. Try to build any expenses—like travel or hosting—into your family budget so you are prepared ahead of time, rather than potentially scrambling later, or finding that you are unable to celebrate in the way you hoped.

This is an ongoing conversation, and your perspectives might change over time. If children are involved, these decisions will impact their experiences as well. Whatever you decide, consider how your holidays and traditions honor God and reflect the things you value most.

 *Surviving the Holidays*

Using the considerations mentioned previously, discuss together how you prefer to handle holidays and family traditions. Identify your top three most important holidays and complete the prompts in the chart.

Partner A

HOLIDAY	HOW/WITH WHOM I WOULD LIKE TO SPEND THIS HOLIDAY	TRADITIONS I'D LIKE TO INCORPORATE (IF APPLICABLE)	THINGS I DO NOT PREFER
1.			
2.			
3.			

Partner B

HOLIDAY	HOW/WITH WHOM I WOULD LIKE TO SPEND THIS HOLIDAY	TRADITIONS I'D LIKE TO INCORPORATE (IF APPLICABLE)	THINGS I DO NOT PREFER
1.			
2.			
3.			

After sharing your charts with each other, come together to discuss the following questions:

- What decisions do you want to make now for how you will handle the holidays discussed?

- What are you most looking forward to related to holidays/traditions?

- How would you like to handle communicating your plans with your families/ friends?

Giving and Receiving Support

There will be times when you will give or receive support from your respective families and friends. This can include emotional support during difficult times, financial support, housing support, caregiving, medical support, and so on. Different types of support might involve just one or both of you. Different people have different levels of comfort when it comes to giving and receiving support.

What's most important when giving support outside your marriage is to make sure both your and your partner's needs are being valued. The support you give to family and friends is determined by your emotions and your capacity and desire to give. Often, we want to help others in our lives who have been there for us, and while our spouse may appreciate that gesture, they may not have the same level of emotional investment. When both your needs are considered, you can make the decision as teammates who care about and value each other's perspectives.

The same holds true when receiving support. When friends or family members step in to help, one person can become offended or struggle with feelings of inadequacy and may not want to accept the help. Have an honest conversation about what it will be like to receive support. Investigate the reasons you might choose to accept or reject help. If it's because of pride, invite the Lord in to guide you, for "'God opposes the proud but shows favor to the humble'" (James 4:6). It may be in your ability to receive help from others that God richly blesses you in your time of need.

 ## *To Give or to Receive?*

For each of the following topics, rate your personal comfort with both giving and receiving support in this area. Partner A will indicate their response with a circle, and Partner B will indicate their response with an asterisk. Then come together and discuss any areas of disagreement. In your conversation, focus on understanding each other's perspective rather than proving your point. For items where an immediate decision needs to be made, come to an agreement. For other items, table the discussion for now and revisit if or when the specific situation arises.

1. Emotional support during difficult times

VERY UNCOMFORTABLE GIVING　　　　　　　　VERY COMFORTABLE GIVING

1　　2　　3　　4　　5　　6　　7　　8　　9　　10

2. Financial support when necessary (bills due, job layoff, debt, etc.)

VERY UNCOMFORTABLE GIVING　　　　　　　　VERY COMFORTABLE GIVING

1　　2　　3　　4　　5　　6　　7　　8　　9　　10

3. Financial support in the form of gifts (for wedding, savings, home purchase, vacation, etc.)

VERY UNCOMFORTABLE GIVING　　　　　　　　VERY COMFORTABLE GIVING

1　　2　　3　　4　　5　　6　　7　　8　　9　　10

4. Housing support (living with family/friends)

VERY UNCOMFORTABLE GIVING　　　　　　　　VERY COMFORTABLE GIVING

1　　2　　3　　4　　5　　6　　7　　8　　9　　10

5. Taking care of family/friends (daily living activities, etc.)

VERY UNCOMFORTABLE GIVING　　　　　　　　VERY COMFORTABLE GIVING

1　　2　　3　　4　　5　　6　　7　　8　　9　　10

6. Medical support (accompanying to medical appointments, making medical decisions, administering treatments, picking up prescriptions, etc.)

VERY UNCOMFORTABLE GIVING   VERY COMFORTABLE GIVING

1   2   3   4   5   6   7   8   9   10

7. Logistical support (home repairs, transportation, mail pickup, etc.)

VERY UNCOMFORTABLE GIVING   VERY COMFORTABLE GIVING

1   2   3   4   5   6   7   8   9   10

As you look at your responses to the preceding items, what can you say about your comfort giving and receiving?

If you find that you have significantly different comfort levels, talk more about what causes you discomfort. Decide if there are any areas where either one of you can compromise a little, or if you can find ways to allow those differences to coexist without creating major issues. If you notice you've reached a total impasse on very critical areas, seek the advice of a coach or a counselor when necessary.

TAKEAWAYS

Your marriage represents a prioritized relationship. Together, with God's direction, you can learn to navigate other relationships with family and friends and leverage them to both give and receive support over the course of your marriage. Committing to putting God and your partner first, will guide you as you make decisions.

Talk It Over

- How does the way you celebrated holidays growing up impact what you'd like to happen now?

- Have you ever needed to receive help in a way that made you uncomfortable? How did you handle the situation, and how did you feel afterward?

- What's something you want to make sure your partner understands when it comes to your relationship with family and friends?

- What relationship, if any, do you expect will be difficult to navigate as you prioritize your marriage?

Keep in Mind

- The relationships you have with friends and family should support the well-being of your marriage, not weaken or threaten it.

- The standards you are used to are not automatic rules in your marriage. Together, you'll need to create new norms that work for you both.

- Many factors impact the level of support you are comfortable giving and receiving. Aim for both of you to feel good about how you navigate these decisions as a team.

Next Steps

- Each of you should write out your own definition of what it looks like to prioritize your marriage. Then, work together to combine them into one. Hang it in a place where you'll see it every day.

- Set aside time at the beginning of each month to revisit any areas where you could not agree on what to do. Find one detail where you do agree and build from there.

- Decide now when you will have any necessary conversations with friends and family based on what you agreed to in this chapter.

CHAPTER 11

Children and Parenting

> *"But as for me and my household, we will serve the Lord."*
>
> JOSHUA 24:15

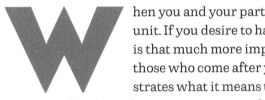hen you and your partner unite in marriage, you form a new family unit. If you desire to have children, your leadership in your family is that much more important because it will chart the course for those who come after you. This scripture from Joshua demonstrates what it means to take a stand for how you want your home to operate. You have the awesome responsibility of setting the tone. Society may offer you one thing; your own parents and family members may offer you something else. At the end of the day, you want God to be the one whose guidance leads you the most.

If you did not grow up in a Christian home, what it looks like to serve the Lord in your family may be new. If you did grow up in a Christian home, you may now have different ideas of what it will mean to raise your family in the faith. It's important that you and your partner establish this for yourselves first. You represent the foundation upon which your future children will grow.

As a couple, you may not always see eye to eye on how to serve and honor the Lord through your family life, either before or after children. You want to identify some essential and basic "to-dos" that you agree to uphold as your standards, like praying each night or reading the Bible each morning. As with many of the other topics discussed in this book, you also want to uncover why these are important to you. You don't always have to agree on every detail, but overall, you do want to find your commonalities and appreciate the perspective each of you has.

How you decide to lead and guide your family determines the experiences you have, the expectations you set, and how your children come to understand the world. It is influenced by your own upbringing, media, traditions, and a range of conscious and unconscious beliefs. When we choose to serve the Lord and give Him the authority over our families, we can rest in this promise from Psalm 32:8: "I will instruct you and teach you in the way you should go; I will counsel you with my loving eye on you." There is no better assurance than to know we are constantly being led and guided by the Lord, as family leaders, parents, and parent-figures to any children He has entrusted to our care.

How You Were Raised

Your childhood experiences form the basis for the beliefs and expectations in your future household. It's important to recognize your own biases and to keep in mind that your partner may have had a different upbringing. As you work together, remember that your goal is to find a path forward that works for your family and equally values what's important to each of you.

While we don't get a vote in how we were raised, we do have more control over how we allow our upbringing to influence our lives as adults. In some instances, you will want the influence of your family to be very present in your marriage and the life you create. The Bible tells us we are to "start children off on the way they should go, and even when they are old they will not turn from it" (Proverbs 22:6). This is a beautiful sentiment, and if our parents were successful in this endeavor, we may want to both honor and replicate that.

In other instances, you may have to intentionally override negative patterns of interaction that don't support the kind of marriage and family you want. Perhaps as an adult you struggle with some issues because your home environment didn't best support your needs. You want to avoid the mistakes of your parents and move forward with strong ideas about how you want your family to operate. God can heal you of whatever challenges you face now because of your upbringing. He can help you overcome any issue that would have a negative impact on your family.

Where You Came From

The following exercise lists several common qualities and characteristics that may have been influenced by how you were raised. For each, consider whether your upbringing had a positive or negative effect on this characteristic. Then, identify how your adult choices are shaped by your childhood experiences (in positive or negative ways) and think about what you'd like to create in your own family. There are two separate charts provided here—one for Partner A and one for Partner B.

Partner A

QUALITY/ CHARACTERISTIC	INFLUENCE FROM MY UPBRINGING	CHOICES I MAKE NOW	WHAT I'D LIKE TO HAPPEN IN OUR FAMILY
Example: Confidence	*Negative influence because my parents didn't affirm my abilities or celebrate me.*	*I affirm myself using God's Word and intentionally think good thoughts about myself.*	*We create affirmation statements for our children and teach them how to think positively about themselves.*
Confidence			
Success			
Trust			
Consistency			
Empathy			
Communication			
Selflessness			
Control			

continued ➡

Partner B

QUALITY/ CHARACTERISTIC	INFLUENCE FROM MY UPBRINGING	CHOICES I MAKE NOW	WHAT I'D LIKE TO HAPPEN IN OUR FAMILY
Confidence			
Success			
Trust			
Consistency			
Empathy			
Communication			
Selflessness			
Control			

Compare your answers in the charts and discuss the following questions:

- Where are we already on the same page regarding ideas for our family?

- How can we best support each other in overriding any negative influences from our upbringings?

- What was most valuable about taking the time to work through this exercise?

Setting Expectations around Having Children

Do you and your partner plan to have children? It's not a simple question. For some, having children together is a primary motivator for being married. But not everyone has the desire for children or feels ready to have them. Some may still be undecided. Some want children very much but have had trouble conceiving. Others may already have children and will enter the marriage as part of a package deal.

So many marriages struggle when couples are not on the same page about this decision or are not completely truthful about their desires, or when one partner is secretly hoping the other person's perspective will change to match theirs. Making this decision from a place of pressure or to placate a partner is not recommended. This is an area of your life where God wants to be deeply involved. After all, He is the ultimate giver of life. Your perspective on these topics may change over time, as your desires and the circumstances in your life change. What's most important is that you create safety and trust in order to share your perspective as candidly as possible, and that you truly understand what your partner wants.

When it comes to having children, there are several aspects to consider, including timing, number of kids, methods of conceiving, and/or adoption. For blended families where children are already part of the equation, considerations include visitation, living arrangements, how to navigate expanding the family, and coparenting, among others. When you dive into the various emotions involved and all the potential outcomes, these are some of the most important decisions you'll make as a couple. Introducing children into a marriage forever changes the relationship, in both wonderful and very challenging ways. It is my prayer that God speaks to you clearly on this issue, and that you lean on His wisdom and power to prepare you and sustain you in whatever conclusion you come to as a couple.

 ## *Planning Your Family*

The following exercise will help you discuss your expectations and make some decisions about having children. For each statement, share your thoughts independently, and then identify how you'd like to proceed as a couple based on what you know right now.

1.   How many children, if any, do you want to have?

Partner A: _____

Partner B: _____

continued ➡

What we've decided _____

2. When would you like to start a family?

Partner A: _____

Partner B: _____

What we've decided _____

3. What are your thoughts about spacing out the ages of children?

Partner A: _____

Partner B: _____

What we've decided _____

4. What would you like to do if you have trouble conceiving children?

Partner A: _____

Partner B: _____

What we've decided _____

5. How do you feel about adoption?

Partner A: _____

Partner B: _____

What we've decided _____

6. If you have children already, how would you like to handle discussing having more children with your current children?

Partner A: _____

Partner B: _____

What we've decided _____

Parenting Styles and Responsibilities

As you consider your role as parents, there are several perspectives that will be helpful. First, remember that children are a reward from the Lord (Psalm 127:3). As such, they truly belong to God. He is entrusting them into your care. He has a plan for their lives, and, as parents, you want to be in alignment with that plan. You should consider yourself a human extension of God's love, and be open to leading and guiding your children in the ways of the Lord.

Second, you will both come with strengths and areas for growth as you raise children together. As you surface differences in this area, consider how both of your approaches are necessary. God has given you the right temperament and characteristics to parent your children well. It's important that you keep in mind the common goal of raising happy, productive, and responsible children. Make peace with the reality that your partner is never going to be the parent that you are, and vice versa.

Third, have realistic and flexible expectations for each of your respective roles and responsibilities. Raising children presents many additional tasks that no one is fully prepared for. Expect your plans and agreements to be adjusted, and speak honestly about what you can and cannot take on. When you find the responsibilities overwhelming, think creatively about how to address your family's needs without one person feeling like everything has to fall on them.

Finally, know that God is with you on this journey. You can rely on His strength, peace, insight, and wisdom. The Bible instructs us, "Trust in the Lord with all your heart and lean not on your own understanding; in all your ways submit to him, and he will make your paths straight" (Proverbs 3:5–6).

What Kind of Parent Are You?

The following exercise will help you uncover your parenting styles and preferences for raising children.

For each of the following scales, select the number that best indicates how you would describe yourself. Partner A should indicate their answers with a circle, and Partner B should use an asterisk. Then, discuss your answers.

1. When it comes to discipline, I am

LESS STRICT   MORE STRICT

1   2   3   4   5   6   7   8   9   10

2. When it comes to rules in our home, I

WANT COMPLIANCE   WANT FLEXIBILITY

1   2   3   4   5   6   7   8   9   10

3. I prefer to spend time with children doing

FUN, LEISURELY THINGS   NECESSARY THINGS

1   2   3   4   5   6   7   8   9   10

4. When it comes to being caring and nurturing, I am

LESS COMFORTABLE   VERY COMFORTABLE

1   2   3   4   5   6   7   8   9   10

5. When it comes to caregiving for children, I expect to be

VERY INVOLVED   INVOLVED IN CERTAIN THINGS

1   2   3   4   5   6   7   8   9   10

6. As parents, being a team works best for me when we

DO THINGS TOGETHER   TAG-TEAM TASKS

1   2   3   4   5   6   7   8   9   10

What potential strengths do you see in how you will work together as parents? What challenges do you anticipate? How will you seek the Lord's guidance in times when you aren't in agreement?

TAKEAWAYS

One of the most important things you'll do as a couple is make decisions about the kind of family you will have. As you follow Christ and seek His wisdom, you'll be able to use your respective backgrounds and strengths to find common ground in this area, and He will guide you as you lead your family on His path.

Talk It Over

- Do you feel ready to have children? Why or why not?

- What are some things you need to work on (individually or jointly) before having children?

- Where do our feelings on children align? Where do they differ?

- What are some issues that raise concerns for you?

- What is our common goal in raising a family together? How do our parenting styles complement each other?

Keep in Mind

- Your upbringing has shaped you in many ways. As you build your own family, be intentional about creating the experience that God has for you.

- It's important to discuss your expectations around having children openly and honestly so that you can be on the same page.

- God is the ultimate parent of all children, and your role will be to guide your children along the path He has set forth for them.

Next Steps

- Ask God to reveal and heal any areas within you that hinder you from being the best for your partner and future children.

- Set a specific date for when you would like to come back to this chapter and continue your discussion. Flag one item for that future conversation.

- Given what you've noticed so far in each other, identify three natural strengths that would make you both great parents.

CHAPTER 12

Expressing Love and Affection

Husbands, love your wives, just as Christ loved the church
and gave himself up for her.

EPHESIANS 5:25

Christ is the perfect example of sacrificial love. In marriage, you will be called to love your spouse, even when it feels hard to do so. When you are frustrated or disappointed, when they don't deserve it, when you are feeling unloved— love is always the answer. While we are not perfect like Jesus, we can strive on this earth to be more like Him every day. This scripture from Ephesians is a great reminder of the depth of love we are to offer our partners in marriage.

When I'm coaching my clients, I am careful to help them understand this motivation—God's call to stretch themselves to demonstrate love to their partner during difficult times. It's important that they have this awareness, because to act in love when you really don't feel like it goes against human nature. When we are upset, we are much more tempted to withdraw or become angry and resentful than to love. This is where the sacrifice is required, but it's also where God's power comes in. We know from 2 Corinthians 12:9 that God's grace is sufficient, and that His power is made perfect in our weakness.

As your relationship grows and evolves, you will need to love each other in different ways and at different levels. When we look at Christ's love as the model, we see that loving someone is a decision and a commitment, even if the feelings don't immediately follow. This is important. For many couples, love comes easily in the beginning of their relationship, and it doesn't require much intentional effort or sacrifice. This is a wonderful and necessary foundation on which to build. I encourage you to revel in it as much as possible. Notice how good and satisfying it feels just to love your partner. It is truly a blessing.

Over time, as situations and issues surface in your marriage, you will be faced with opportunities to make critical choices. Will you hold on to the past, criticize mistakes, and fall back on your old way of being, or will you choose to love? Notice that in this scripture, there is an exchange being made. Christ gave himself up to demonstrate His love. In your marriage there will be times where you are the only one preventing yourself from choosing love. But when love is your primary focus, sacrificing a part of yourself, your pride, your hurt, and your anger will be well worth the exchange.

Speaking Each Other's Love Languages

In the book *The 5 Love Languages* by Gary Chapman, we learn about the various ways people best receive and express love: acts of service, physical touch, quality time, giving gifts, and words of affirmation. This concept resonates with many couples, as your preferred love language constantly shapes your experience with your partner.

Most couples have different love languages, but this helps you expand your capacity to give and receive love. When you are only thinking about giving and receiving love in one way, you become conditioned to believe that is the only way (or the best way). But love is one of the most abundant and ever-available things in the world. Love is all around you all the time. You only need to be able to translate love in its many forms to make it tangible for you.

In marriage, the love you share with your partner is a gift. Just as you might select a physical gift based on their preferences, choose everyday expressions of love in the same way. This will often require that you stretch yourself in ways that may feel a little unfamiliar. Why might you want to speak your partner's love language when it's not the same as yours?

There will be times you will need to lean on God to help you love and receive love from your spouse well. It may be difficult to interpret some of your partner's actions as acts of love if it isn't how you're used to offering it. As you continue to grow, be mindful of valuing what your partner is offering. There may be a temptation to use the concept of love languages against each other, demanding that your partner "prove" their love to you in specific ways. This sets up unrealistic expectations and leads to frustration. No one but God can love you perfectly. You want to share love in a way that is full of grace, compassion, and understanding for where you are both still learning.

Value Your Partner

The following exercise will help you discuss and better understand each other's love languages. Complete the following statements and discuss your answers with your partner. As you listen to each other, keep in mind how you can understand, value, and respond to your partner's preferences.

1. The things that matter the most to me when it comes to feeling loved include:

Partner A: _____

Partner B: _____

2. It's important to me that I speak your love language because:

Partner A: _____

Partner B: _____

3. When I have a hard time expressing love to you, I will:

Partner A: _____

Partner B: _____

4. When you want to feel more loved by me, the best way to approach me is:

Partner A: _____

Partner B: _____

5. One way we can keep our love languages at the front of our minds is to:

Partner A: _____

Partner B: _____

Affection and Gratitude

Marriage should be a safe place where you feel valued, appreciated, and cared for. Yet it can sometimes be easy to take each other for granted. God's Word reminds us to express affection and gratitude for each other in 1 Thessalonians 5:11: "Therefore encourage one another and build each other up." It's tempting to believe those closest to you always know how much you value them. But demonstrating affection and gratitude is a very healthy practice to build into your relationship.

As with your love languages, each of you may have a different approach to expressing affection and practicing gratitude. There is no one right way. There are just two hearts that want to connect and recognize the blessing that you each represent in one another's lives. Affection can be expressed verbally (using terms of endearment or a loving, sweet tone) and through physical touch (kissing, hugging, holding hands). In your marriage, you want to both give and receive affection in as many ways as possible. God created us to connect with each other. The affection you show your partner is a gift that you give to them.

In the hustle of achieving goals, it's helpful to pause to celebrate, affirm, and give thanks for what God is doing in your lives. It is often in these moments that you can see your growth as individuals and as a couple. Being able to recognize this early on will help you appreciate future blessings to come.

 Ask for What You Need

We all have different values and priorities. The following exercise will help your partner learn which expressions of affection and gratitude are most important to you. This builds on the idea of love languages and how we respond to different ways of showing love. Rank each of the following ten items in order of how important it is that your partner show affection and/or express their gratitude to you in this way.

Partner A   Partner B

Partner A	Partner B	
		When I reach a goal or accomplishment at work, I want you to congratulate and celebrate with me.
		When I take care of an extra responsibility around the house, I want you to express your gratitude.
		When I cook a good meal, I want you to let me know you appreciate it.
		When I do something nice just for you, I'd like you to show me affection.
		When I make a sacrifice of my time, I want you to notice and say thank you.
		When I am there to support you emotionally, I'd like you to let me know you appreciate it.
		When we see each other at the end of the day, I'd like a hug and/or kiss.
		When I'm feeling afraid or sad, I'd like you to comfort me.
		When I'm having a hard day, I'd appreciate your encouragement or affection.
		When we have an argument and make up, I'd like to show each other affection.

After sharing your answers to the preceding prompts, what do you notice about your preferences for affection and gratitude? Where do you differ the most? Where do you agree? What will you do to ensure the expression of affection and gratitude is something that works for both of you?

If God is the model of sacrificial love, how will His example guide you both in this area?

TAKEAWAYS

In the early relationship stages, it can be easier to be effusive in the way you love and appreciate each other. As your lives change over time, it can be easy to lose sight of this important element that makes your relationship feel rewarding. Using Christ as your model of sacrifice can help you love your partner the way they need to be loved—and help them love you that way in return.

Talk It Over

- When was a time you felt most loved by your partner? What made it so special to you?

- Given your different love languages, what will each of you need to be intentional about doing?

- When you are not experiencing the kind of love and affection you desire, how will you communicate that to each other?

- What's one thing you now know a little better about your partner after going through this chapter together?

Keep in Mind

- Each of you has different ways you prefer to give and receive love; knowing your love languages expands how you can demonstrate love in your relationship.

- Affection and gratitude are important components in helping you stay connected and feel valued.

- When both of you are responsive to each other's preferences for love and affection, your relationship will thrive.

Next Steps

- Create a list of three things you can do to express love to your partner in ways they receive it best.

- Take time at the end of each day to pause and show affection (hold hands, hug, cuddle) and express at least one thing you appreciate about each other.

- Include in your prayer time each week a request that God will continue to give you insight and awareness for how to love each other well.

CHAPTER 13

Sex

> *Do not deprive each other except perhaps by mutual consent and for a time, so that you may devote yourselves to prayer. Then come together again so that Satan will not tempt you because of your lack of self-control.*
>
> **1 CORINTHIANS 7:5**

For the married couple, sex is a gift you share with each other. It is the means by which you come together to create new life in your family. It is how you express your passion and desire for each other. It is a sacred way to express your love.

While physical intimacy is a gift, it can be one of those issues that creates division and conflict among couples. Each of us comes to marriage with different beliefs, experiences, and expectations relating to sex. We have different preferences, desires, and drives. I believe these differences can open the door to some of the most profound and vulnerable conversations partners can have together.

The preceding scripture highlights that sex within marriage should be a mutual experience that you freely talk about. It's not something that, when absent in a marriage, should be avoided in discussion. Likewise, if your sex life is not what you'd like it to be, it's important to come together and find common ground.

There is no right amount of sex for a couple to have. What matters most is that you both account for each other's desires and find ways to make this aspect of your relationship work. This is an area of great temptation, so the more you communicate honestly and openly about where you stand and your level of satisfaction, the stronger you make your marriage. You also strengthen your ability to remain sexually faithful.

We've all heard stories of sex being used as a weapon in marriage. One person may deprive the other out of anger and resentment. One person may overtly pressure the other out of their own selfish desires. One person may make sexual demands that don't honor the marriage covenant. One person may engage in sex only for their satisfaction and neglect the needs of their partner. As you consider sexual intimacy in your relationship, it's important to assess where your wants, needs, and desires are coming from. What experiences and assumptions might be influencing you? Would God be pleased? Does it honor the type of partner you want to be?

There may be times where having sex in your marriage is legitimately not possible or healthy. As a couple, you want to talk about this, communicating what you expect and how you will operate during these periods. Remember, while sex is an important part of marriage, it's not the only part of marriage. There are many ways you can be physically intimate and maintain that part of your relationship.

Like all things in your life, sex is something you can take to God in prayer. He wants to be intimately involved in every area of your marriage. He understands your needs and desires. He wants you to experience the intimacy and pleasure that come from having a satisfying sex life. He designed you and your partner to be able to express your love in this exclusive way.

Establishing Your Comfort Level

What is your comfort level with sex? Our comfort level is shaped by our childhood experiences, messages we hear in society and the media, and a host of other factors that might not be in your control. Few people take the time to pause and actually consider what has influenced their thoughts about sex. But when you understand what's been driving your relationship with sex, you have the opportunity to ensure it's what you want it to be.

If you find yourself fearful about sex, I want you to know you can change it. You may have endured sexual abuse or received messages that sex is a bad thing. If you have a lot of shame around sex, that is also something that can be worked through to create a more fulfilling experience. Alternatively, if you find you have few sexual boundaries, you may want to explore that further. That could also be a sign of emotional voids or other trauma. God can heal any negative experience that gets in the way of you having a fulfilling sexual relationship with your partner.

Be honest with yourself regarding your feelings about sex. If you have any negative emotions, bring them to the Lord. Ask for His insight and wisdom, and don't hesitate to get professional counseling or coaching on these issues. See your partner as an advocate and support system if you struggle with sex in any way. Even if you have dramatically different comfort levels, you both are coming together to have this aspect of your relationship thrive as much as any other area.

What Are You Comfortable With?

The following exercise will help you open up the lines of communication regarding your comfort level with sex. Answer each of the following questions, using the sections for Partner A and Partner B. Then, come together and discuss your responses with each other, reflecting on what you've learned and reaching agreements where possible. During your conversation, try to listen to each other without judgment or agenda. This is a wonderful opportunity to understand each other and create a safe space for vulnerable communication.

Partner A

1. When it comes to sex, what are you very comfortable with?

_____

_____

2. When it comes to sex, what do you get a little worried about?

_____

_____

3. What are some bad experiences you've had with sex or negative messages you've received?

_____

_____

4. When you think about sex in your marriage, what do you want to make sure of?

_____

_____

continued ➡

5. Complete this sentence: Sometimes, sex for me can be . . .

_____

_____

6. What do you need in order to feel sexually intimate with your partner?

_____

_____

7. When are you most comfortable being sexually intimate?

_____

_____

8. When you think about being comfortable involving God in this aspect of your marriage, what does that look like?

_____

_____

Partner B

1. When it comes to sex, what are you very comfortable with?

_____

_____

2. When it comes to sex, what do you get a little worried about?

_____

_____

3. What are some bad experiences you've had with sex or negative messages you've received?

_____

_____

4. When you think about sex in your marriage, what do you want to make sure of?

_____

_____

5. Complete this sentence: Sometimes, sex for me can be . . .

_____

_____

6. What do you need in order to feel sexually intimate with your partner?

_____

_____

7. When are you most comfortable being sexually intimate?

_____

_____

8. When you think about being comfortable involving God in this aspect of your marriage, what does that look like?

_____

_____

Understanding Each Other's Preferences and Expectations

Each person comes to a marriage with their individual preferences and expectations around sex. At times, you may uncover a preference or expectation you were not previously aware of. The way you operate sexually as a couple will grow and evolve just like other areas of your relationship.

As you might expect here, communication is key. Because our preferences are based on many things that have nothing to do with our partners, it's important that you understand yourself enough to be able to effectively communicate what your partner needs to know. What do you need your partner to express and communicate to you in your sexual relationship? How do you see your expectations having a positive influence on your relationship? Are there any preferences you have that might not be best for your marriage? The more self-aware you are, the more deeply you'll be able to explain what's important to you. If you have any confusion or blind spots, God is there to help you see what you need to see.

Your goal should be to respond to your partner rather than judging them. Your willingness to understand will set the tone for how honestly you are able to communicate about this topic. One person's preferences are not more important than another's. As you discuss preferences and expectations, test them against what God would want for you both. Sex in marriage is a sacred experience, and you both want to be on the same page about what that looks like for you.

 *Share Your Preferences*

The following exercise will help you share any preferences or expectations you have related to sex and physical intimacy right now. Respond to each item listed in the column on the left, sharing your honest thoughts, preferences, and expectations. If during this conversation, you make some mutually agreed upon decisions, write them down in the third column. Feel free to discuss additional items that are not included.

PREFERENCE/EXPECTATION	PARTNER A	PARTNER B	ANY MUTUALLY AGREED DECISIONS
How often I'd like to have sex			
The time of day I prefer to have sex			
My preferences around foreplay			

Things I really enjoy during sex			
Things I don't like during sex			
How I like for sex to be initiated			
The best way to approach me about any sexual concerns			
How I want to deal with any sexual attraction to another person			
How I will communicate when I'm not in the mood for sex			
Something I've always wanted to try			
My thoughts about watching pornography			

Voicing Your Desires

How comfortable do you feel communicating what you want? How a person communicates their desires is often based on how they believe their partner will respond. At times, you might become so preoccupied with what your partner will think or feel that you diminish what's actually true for you. In your marriage, you want to be authentic—the best and fullest version of yourself. We are not often taught how to voice our desires in a way that both honors who we are *and* is respectful of our partners.

As you communicate your desires, be careful not to do so from a negative place. For example, do you say, "You never _____ (fill in the blank with something you want them to do)"? Or, have you said in a harsh tone, "I really wish you would _____ (fill in the blank with something you've asked for numerous times)"? This comes out of frustration when you feel that what you want is being overlooked or dismissed.

In marriage, you want to cultivate the belief that you both want the same thing. It may look very different, and you may have different approaches, but, at the end of the day, you both want to be in a relationship that is happy, mutually beneficial, and fulfilling. You want to feel valued, appreciated, and cared for. You want to feel desired and admired. When you believe that your partner wants the same thing for you, voicing your desires becomes a much more comfortable experience. You are coming together to create a new united self. It requires honesty. When you deny what you really want, you don't give your partner the chance to love all of you.

 ## *What Are Your Desires, Anyway?*

The following exercise will help both of you voice your desires at a deeper level. To start, let's take a big picture view of the experience you want to have related to sex.

1. I'd like sex between us to be:

Partner A: _____

Partner B: _____

2. I'd describe my experience with sex as:

Partner A: _____

Partner B: _____

For each of the following desires, rate how much you enjoy these things as part of your sexual encounters on a scale of 1–10. Partner A can indicate their answers by circling their responses, and Partner B can place an asterisk next to their responses. If you are unsure about your desires for a certain item, feel free to check the box "unsure" and you and your partner can explore this area together over the course of your marriage.

1. Being told you are desired during sex

NOT VERY ENJOYABLE									VERY ENJOYABLE	UNSURE
1	2	3	4	5	6	7	8	9	10	☐

2. Seeing each other's bodies during sex

NOT VERY ENJOYABLE									VERY ENJOYABLE	UNSURE
1	2	3	4	5	6	7	8	9	10	☐

3. Audible enjoyment during sex (talking, moaning)

NOT VERY ENJOYABLE									VERY ENJOYABLE	UNSURE
1	2	3	4	5	6	7	8	9	10	☐

4. Making eye contact during sex

NOT VERY
ENJOYABLE

VERY
ENJOYABLE

UNSURE

1   2   3   4   5   6   7   8   9   10

5. Kissing before, during, and/or after sex

NOT VERY
ENJOYABLE

VERY
ENJOYABLE

UNSURE

1   2   3   4   5   6   7   8   9   10

6. Mutual orgasm (one after the other or at the same time)

NOT VERY
ENJOYABLE

VERY
ENJOYABLE

UNSURE

1   2   3   4   5   6   7   8   9   10

7. Cuddling before, during, and/or after sex

NOT VERY
ENJOYABLE

VERY
ENJOYABLE

UNSURE

1   2   3   4   5   6   7   8   9   10

8. Sexy lingerie

NOT VERY
ENJOYABLE

VERY
ENJOYABLE

UNSURE

1   2   3   4   5   6   7   8   9   10

9. Toys or other items during sex

NOT VERY
ENJOYABLE

VERY
ENJOYABLE

UNSURE

1   2   3   4   5   6   7   8   9   10

10. Role play

NOT VERY
ENJOYABLE

VERY
ENJOYABLE

UNSURE

1   2   3   4   5   6   7   8   9   10

After completing this exercise, discuss the following questions:

• What was it like to have a conversation about sex in this way?

• What's something you learned about each other that will be helpful in your marriage?

• How can you keep the lines of communication open on this topic?

TAKEAWAYS

Your sexual experiences as a couple will grow and evolve over time. Physical intimacy is an important way to express God's love toward your partner. It's important to come to this conversation honestly so you can give one another this gift in the most fulfilling ways.

Talk It Over

- Where are you already on the same page about in this aspect of your relationship?

- What concerns do you have that you still might need to work through?

- How might you want to approach sex differently based on what you've learned about each other?

- How would you jointly define a very satisfying sex life for yourselves as a couple?

Keep in Mind

- Sexual intimacy in your marriage is a gift that both of you should find enjoyable and fulfilling.

- Any barriers to you enjoying your sexual relationship together can be overcome and worked through.

- Your relationship is a safe space for you to share your sexual desires and honor the gift that sex is to your marriage.

Next Steps

- Make talking about sex a regular part of your conversations. Set a monthly date night to discuss your relationship and be sure sex is a part of that conversation.

- Remember that your needs and desires are both equally important. When your partner asks your opinion, be honest. If there is something you want to talk about, identify the most comfortable way for you to bring it up.

- Seek God's help through prayer if you are struggling with any negative or destructive beliefs or thoughts about sex with your partner. Reach out to a professional if this is significantly impacting your relationship.

CHAPTER 14

Growing Spiritually Together

> *Let the message of Christ dwell among you richly as you teach and admonish one another with all wisdom through psalms, hymns, and songs from the Spirit, singing to God with gratitude in your hearts. And whatever you do, whether in word or deed, do it all in the name of the Lord Jesus, giving thanks to God the Father through him.*
>
> **COLOSSIANS 3:16–17**

Your union is the opportunity to grow together in every aspect of your life. The success of the marriage you build together rests on your spiritual foundation. Your spiritual growth as individuals and as a couple is a humbling experience that directs you to a deeper relationship with God. The greater the depths of that relationship, the more you come to know who you are in Christ; the more you know who you are in Christ, the more unconditional love you can offer your spouse.

As believers, you probably already expect to be on the same page about spiritual growth. But many people don't know that it is normal to experience ebbs and flows of spiritual growth and stagnation. I offer this to you so that when it happens, you don't fall into the belief that something has gone wrong or start shaming yourself or your partner.

God's love and pursuit of you are unconditional. He already knows when you'll be most intimately connected to Him and when your heart will stray or question. He is the steady constant in your relationship. That's good news, because you can rest in the peace that nothing will ever separate you from His love (Romans 8:38–39).

In your marriage, you want your spiritual connection to be a source of joy and gratitude. Be careful not to judge each other's spiritual progress, but instead encourage one another with the love of God. There is no more profound and inspiring force than love. Your marriage is not the place for you to be on a spiritual high horse; it's the place where you support each other in becoming the individuals and the couple God created you to be.

When the message of Christ dwells among you richly, you constantly seek the greatest good for each other. Your growth as you strive for a deeper relationship with God is born out of gratitude for who He is in your life. Your individual experiences reveal different levels of your understanding and recognition of who God is. Sometimes your experiences will coincide with your partner's; other times they will not. Still, you are both right on track, and God is providing the necessary experiences you need to step into the life He has set aside for you. Trusting Him in the process and pace of your spiritual growth will be extremely important throughout your married life.

Spiritual History and Habits

Where you are in your spiritual journey is partly a function of all the things that have happened previously. It's important that you both honor and appreciate your spiritual history because it was a necessary path that led you to where you are now. For some individuals, growing up in a home where they were taught about God was very normal, and having a spiritual growth focus may be second nature. For others, the walk with God may be relatively new, perhaps even counter to how their family of origin operates. If this is your experience, it never has to hold you back in terms of what's possible in your spiritual growth. God never makes mistakes. If you continue to seek Him, He won't allow anything to happen that would throw you off course for the plan He has for you.

As you come together to explore what spiritual growth will look like in your marriage, there's no need to feel shame or to feel like you are on unequal footing. What's most important now is that you are headed in the same direction from this point forward. You have the opportunity to create whatever spiritual habits will serve the life God is calling you to live.

What's great about habits is that they can quickly become part of your identity. Actions repeated over time become part of your way of operating. When you think about your spiritual life and relationship with God, what things would you like to just be your way of life? What are rituals would you like to not even think twice about? You have the wonderful opportunity to create that for yourself and your marriage right now.

Raised in the Faith

The following exercise will help you both understand your own spiritual backgrounds and how your upbringing influences the decisions and habits you'd like to implement now as a couple. Complete the following statements and discuss your answers.

1. Growing up, my family:

Partner A: _____

Partner B: _____

2. In my house we never or always:

Partner A: _____

Partner B: _____

3. As a child, I would have described God as:

Partner A: _____

Partner B: _____

4. When I think about how I'd like our family to see God, I want to make sure:

Partner A: _____

Partner B: _____

5. I would describe my own personal relationship with God as being:

Partner A: _____

Partner B: _____

continued ➡

6. The most important spiritual habits for me are:

Partner A: _____

Partner B: _____

7. For me, spiritual growth would look like:

Partner A: _____

Partner B: _____

Now discuss which habits you want to bring to your marriage, and which, if any, you'd like to leave behind.

The Couple That Prays Together . . .

You've probably heard the old adage, "The couple that prays together, stays together." If you endorse this view, why do you think this is true? What separates couples who pray from those who don't? I would argue that the action of praying together comes from a set of common beliefs that have united the couple under a common goal: to acknowledge and tap into the power that God readily provides for you to live the abundant life He has promised.

There is nothing you'll experience in your marriage that God has not already equipped you to handle. He loves you and values your marriage that much. When both you and your partner are of the same mindset in this regard, there is no obstacle the two of you can't overcome with God's help. Prayer is a key tool you have available in ensuring your marriage succeeds.

It's important that you both keep your individual relationships with God while also creating a unique relationship as a triad. Your decisions of when, how, and what to take to God as a couple may shift and evolve over time. For now, think about the areas in your relationship where you want God's input, wisdom, and guidance. Think about how each of you might hear from God in different ways and how you'll come together to share what you receive from Him.

Being intentional about setting aside time to pray early on in your marriage will make it a natural habit for the future. The more you involve God during these initial years, the more you invite His hand to shape your later years. God is all-knowing, and through regular prayer, you'll be able to tap into this power.

 # *Achieving God's Purpose*

God's Word provides an amazing guide for prayer. God has promised us that His Word "will not return to me empty, but will accomplish what I desire and achieve the purpose for which I sent it" (Isaiah 55:11). Using scripture is a wonderful foundation for your prayer life as a couple. The following exercise will help you identify scriptures that resonate with you and illuminate the topics we've covered throughout this book. For each topic listed, circle (Partner A) or place an asterisk beside (Partner B) the one that speaks to you the most. Feel free to add others not listed here.

A scripture I will use to help guide me in being a great partner:

> *Guide me in your truth and teach me, for you are God my Savior, and my hope is in you all day long.* (PSALM 25:5)

....

> *May these words of my mouth and this meditation of my heart be pleasing in your sight, Lord, my Rock and my Redeemer.* (PSALM 19:14)

....

> *Be devoted to one another in love. Honor one another above yourselves.* (ROMANS 12:10)

....

_____

_____

_____

A scripture that will help keep us grounded as a couple:

> *Finally, brothers and sisters, rejoice! Strive for full restoration, encourage one another, be of one mind, live in peace. And the God of love and peace will be with you.* (2 CORINTHIANS 13:11)

....

continued ➡

Though one may be overpowered, two can defend themselves. A cord of three strands is not quickly broken. (ECCLESIASTES 4:12)

....

Therefore, as God's chosen people, holy and dearly loved, clothe yourselves with compassion, kindness, humility, gentleness and patience. Bear with each other and forgive one another if any of you has a grievance against someone. Forgive as the Lord forgave you. And over all these virtues put on love, which binds them all together in perfect unity. (COLOSSIANS 3:12–14)

....

_____

_____

_____

A scripture that will guide us in navigating our differences:

Let the morning bring me word of your unfailing love, for I have put my trust in you. Show me the way I should go, for to you I entrust my life.
(PSALM 143:8)

....

Be completely humble and gentle; be patient, bearing with one another in love. Make every effort to keep the unity of the Spirit through the bond of peace.
(EPHESIANS 4:2–3)

....

Get rid of all bitterness, rage and anger, brawling and slander, along with every form of malice. Be kind and compassionate to one another, forgiving each other, just as in Christ God forgave you. (EPHESIANS 4:31–32)

....

_____

_____

_____

_____

A scripture that will help us keep our marriage full of love:

> *Do everything in love. (1 CORINTHIANS 16:14)*

....

> *Love is patient, love is kind. It does not envy, it does not boast, it is not proud. It does not dishonor others, it is not self-seeking, it is not easily angered, it keeps no record of wrongs. Love does not delight in evil but rejoices with the truth. It always protects, always trusts, always hopes, always perseveres. Love never fails. (1 CORINTHIANS 13:4–8)*

....

> *Above all, love each other deeply, because love covers over a multitude of sins. (1 PETER 4:8)*

....

_____

_____

_____

After choosing a scripture for each prompt, discuss these questions:

- What is the value of sharing scripture with each other?

- Why are scripture and prayer important in building a foundation for your marriage?

- How will you keep these scriptures at the forefront of your mind?

TAKEAWAYS

As with so many of the other topics covered in this book, your spirituality as a couple will grow and evolve as you have new experiences together. No matter where you find yourself at any given moment in time, God is always there, reaching out to support and guide you.

Talk It Over

- What was the most valuable part of this chapter for you?

- What's something that you had not considered before?

- How are you feeling about this area of your relationship?

- What questions still remain for you to discuss later?

- How have you already gotten off to a great start in this area?

Keep in Mind

- Your spiritual walk, individually and as a couple, forms the foundation of your marriage.

- Through prayer and relationship with God, you have access to wisdom and guidance to help you make good decisions.

- Maintaining your individual relationship with God is just as valuable as having a relationship with Him as a couple.

Next Steps

- Identify one to three baseline habits to support your spiritual development, and commit to doing those things no matter what.

- Decide now that when one of you cannot pray to God about a certain issue, the other will step in and intercede.

- Set aside regular intervals (two to four times per year) to assess your spiritual growth.

A FINAL WORD

Congratulations! God is smiling down on you. Your commitment to starting your marriage off with a strong foundation is something to celebrate. Your willingness to look at yourselves and one another with a desire to understand and come together is an essential ingredient in making your marriage a success. I'm so happy for you.

The time and effort you have invested in going through this book will yield wonderful rewards for your relationship. You have saved yourself unnecessary confusion and time wasted with unrealistic expectations. You now have the opportunity to enter your marriage with your eyes wide open and fixed on the Lord. Because you have sought His wisdom and insight during this process, you understand just how active and involved He wants to be in your union. In Proverbs 8:17 we are told this of God: "I love those who love me, and those who seek me find me." It is love that led you to do this work together, and God is showering His love on you. It is my prayer that your marriage be filled with good fruit, as you have planted valuable seeds together here in this book.

RESOURCES

The 5 Love Languages: The Secret to Love that Lasts by Gary Chapman: Offers in-depth discussion and assessment of how individuals best give and receive love in relationships.

Communication Miracles for Couples: Easy and Effective Tools to Create More Love and Less Conflict by Jonathan Robinson: Provides concrete tools to improve communication.

Desperate Marriages: Moving Toward Hope and Healing in Your Relationship by Gary Chapman: Offers a valuable perspective for how to navigate challenging times in marriage.

How We Love: Discover Your Love Style, Enhance Your Marriage by Milan Yerkovich and Kay Yerkovich: Makes the connection between childhood upbringing and how it influences the challenges couples face in relationships.

Love Marriage Again with Dr. Chavonne podcast: An engaging and relatable podcast that provides tools and coaching exercises to help couples love each other well.

Loving What Is: Four Questions that Can Change Your Life by Byron Katie and Stephen Mitchell: Presents a valuable framework for asking questions that create positive shifts in your relationship and in your life.

Making Marriage Simple: Ten Relationship-Saving Truths by Harville Hendrix and Helen LaKelly Hunt: Practical perspectives that help couples get along better and enjoy marriage with less conflict and stress.

Non-Violent Communication: Create Your Life, Your Relationships, and Your World in Harmony with Your Values by Marshall Rosenberg: Valuable perspective on how to communicate from a place of vulnerability, peace, and calm.

Questions for Couples Journal: 400 Questions to Enjoy, Reflect, and Connect with Your Partner by Maggie Reyes: Offers engaging questions to deepen conversation and connection in your relationship.

Voices in Your Ear: New Conversations to Renew Your Mind and Transform Your Marriage by Dr. Chavonne Perotte: A devotional for women focused on ten principles to create a better marriage.

Why Talking Is Not Enough: Eight Loving Actions That Will Transform Your Marriage by Susan Page: Action-oriented tools that approach marriage improvement as a spiritual growth journey.

REFERENCES

Chapman, Gary. *The 5 Love Languages*. Walker Large Print, 2010. First published 1992.

Kolmar, Chris. "Average Number of Jobs in a Lifetime [2021]: All Statistics." Zippia. May 19, 2021. Zippia.com/advice/average-number-jobs-in-lifetime/#:~:text=After %20extensive%20research%2C%20our%20data,years%20as%20of%20January %202020.

INDEX

Acknowledgments

First, I acknowledge the Lord for sending me the right ideas to share throughout this book. When we are weak, He is strong. I'm so grateful for the bursts of wisdom He graciously gave me to share with you.

Thank you to my husband and parents for their support in writing this book. Your willingness to step in and help out at home so I could focus and write meant so much to me. Thanks also to my friends and family who have supported my work. I'm so grateful. Special thanks to Maggie Reyes, my biggest cheerleader; Jennifer Brown, for your encouragement; and Kristen Finch, for just being in my life. I'm also grateful for my coaches and spiritual leaders who've influenced me.

About the Author

 **Dr. Chavonne Perotte** is a life and marriage coach who helps couples love each other well. She believes the quickest path to improving a marriage starts with assessing the ways we as individuals can think differently, grow, and evolve and then come together better as a couple. Dr. Chavonne provides virtual coaching to couples all over the world seeking a combination of Christian-faith guidance and transformational coaching tools.

She received her doctorate from the Johns Hopkins Bloomberg School of Public Health and focused her research on communication and intimate partnerships. She is the author of *Voices in Your Ear: New Conversations to Transform Your Mind and Renew Your Marriage*. To learn more, access free resources, and to work with Dr. Chavonne directly, visit her website at DrChavonne.com, or follow her on Instagram @chavonneperotte.